# Creating Financially
# Sustainable Congregations

# Creating Financially Sustainable Congregations

## James L. Elrod Jr.

CHURCH
PUBLISHING
INCORPORATED

Church Publishing
19 East 34th Street
New York, NY 10016
www.churchpublishing.org

Cover design by Jennifer Kopec, 2Pug Design
Typeset by Denise Hoff

Library of Congress Cataloging-in-Publication Data

Names: Elrod, James L., author.
Title: Creating financially sustainable congregations / James L. Elrod Jr.
Description: New York, NY : Church Publishing, [2021] | Includes
   bibliographical references.
Identifiers: LCCN 2021000120 (print) | LCCN 2021000121 (ebook) | ISBN
   9781640652873 (paperback) | ISBN 9781640652880 (epub)
Subjects: LCSH: Church finance.
Classification: LCC BV770 .E47 2021 (print) | LCC BV770 (ebook) | DDC
   254/.8--dc23
LC record available at https://lccn.loc.gov/2021000120
LC ebook record available at https://lccn.loc.gov/2021000121

# Contents

# Preface

*This book is for clergy, lay leaders, and church members* who have decided that when it comes to money and church, avoiding hard conversations is no longer acceptable.[1] It is a book for those who realize the task of bringing into place a financial infrastructure capable of sustaining their church is ultimately their responsibility and they want to do something about it. Whether their most pressing problem is securing space in an industrial park to plant a new church or creating a realistic budget, certain bedrock financial principles always apply. *Creating Financially Sustainable Congregations* can help facilitate more productive conversations among church leaders about what is required to create or recreate a financially sustainable church in the third decade of the twenty-first century.

This book will give some readers a better sense of the context in which churches operate in this new millennium. Much has changed in the first two decades of the twenty-first century in the area of church finance. The playbook on church financial matters that served many churches well during the final decades of the twentieth century has become obsolete. *Creating Financially Sustainable Congregations* is an update from the front, aimed at providing church leaders with information they need to set their financial house in order and position their church for success.

The challenges brought on by these structural changes in church finance have been amplified by a series of external economic shocks. As this text goes to press, the pandemic of Covid-19 rages on. During 2020, Covid-19 profoundly and negatively affected fundraising for many churches. This threat to their primary source of revenue has obvi-

---

1  *Lay leaders* refers to nonordained church members who serve their congregation in a voluntary leadership capacity. This includes, but is not limited to, service on the governing board or council of the church. *Church leaders* refers to clergy, staff, and lay leaders collectively.

ous implications for a congregation's near-term financial stability. And yet doing what's necessary just to keep the doors open isn't enough. How can a church respond to immediate financial threats while simultaneously bringing into place the processes and systems that will better position it to flourish once today's crisis has passed?

## What You'll Find Inside

Chapter 1 explains why church leaders often find it difficult to discuss their congregation's financial situation. Most clergy do not receive formal training in financial matters. Lay leaders who may be familiar with commercial financial issues don't appreciate the peculiarities of the nonprofit financial world in which a church operates. Consequently, conversations among church leaders regarding financial matters can be disjointed and unproductive. This situation needs to be acknowledged before it can be resolved.

Chapter 2 describes differences in terminology that can make financial conversations about churches difficult. Unlike other nonprofit organizations, churches aren't required to report their financial results to the federal government. This means there is no comprehensive, accessible database on church financial performance. With no comprehensive, accessible database, church leaders find comparing the performance of their church to others is often impossible.

Chapter 3 is an overview of essential nonprofit accounting and reporting practices. This chapter was written for clergy and lay leaders who have no formal training in finance. You will learn how the four basic financial reports that comprise the audited financial statements of a church work and how they interact with one another. Standard financial information, however, may not tell the full story of a congregation's financial journey. Church leaders need to consider whether their church would benefit by creating additional content and distributing financial information beyond what's required.

Chapter 4 describes how a church accesses financial capital so it can grow its mission. Churches, like other nonprofit organizations, have limited access to outside capital. Understanding the challenges churches face in creating permanent capital is the key to understanding what must be done to create a financially sustainable enterprise.

Chapter 5 highlights the issues churches encounter with budgets and budgeting. Nimi Wariboko, a former faculty member at Andover Newton Seminary, famously proclaims, "Budget is theology."[2] A budget describes a congregation's near-term plan for living life together in faith. The process of budgeting, not just the budget document itself, is an integral part of a sustainable mission and an act of faith. Budgets and budgeting are critical contributors to the process of building the church's permanent capital base discussed in chapter 4.

Chapter 6 describes today's philanthropic landscape. Americans are among the world's most generous people. How Americans express that generosity, however, is changing. The percentage of gifts to religious organizations continues to decline. Moreover, the philanthropic landscape itself is changing rapidly. The consequences for church fundraising over the next ten years will be profound.

Chapter 7 considers generational differences in charitable giving. It is closely linked to some of the developments highlighted in chapter 6. The so-called Baby Boom generation provides the majority of the financial support to nonprofit organizations today. This will no longer be true by 2030. How does a church maintain the financial engagement of its Boomer members, whose gifts keep the doors open today, while cultivating the financial support of Gen Xer members, whose gifts will be the key to maintaining financial sustainability in the not-too-distant future?

Chapter 8 highlights the special challenges encountered by churches in financial crisis. As church leaders who lived through the coronavirus pandemic learned, financial crises experienced by a church often begin outside the church walls. A church can't immunize itself from financial crisis because the crisis is the byproduct of events outside the church's control. Successfully managing through a financial crisis calls for a different style of leadership than what's needed during times of financial stability.

Chapter 9 addresses the question confronting church leadership in all times and places: how to create a sustainable financial infrastructure so that the church can realize its mission today and in the future.

---

2 Nimi Wariboko, *Accounting and Money for Ministerial Leadership* (Eugene, OR: Wipf & Stock, 2013), 66.

Financial sustainability and missional sustainability are two sides of the same coin. What must church leaders do to make sure their congregation takes the necessary steps to address both?

## Who Made This Book Possible

I hope this book contributes to your understanding of what's required to create and maintain a financially sustainable church. If it does, it's because a number of individuals have shared their insights on nonprofit financial matters. These include Gary Bewkes, Lynn Birdsong, Rev. Jack Bishop, Rev. Beth Blunt, Daniel Cain, Rebecca Chopp, Obie Clifford, Murray Decock, the Rt. Rev. Ian Douglas, Duncan Edwards, Forman Friend, Neil Grabois, Sister Grace Marie Hiltz, Rev. Jim Lemler, Linda Lorimer, Stephanie Ratcliffe, Greg Sterling, Lydia Stevens, Pam Wesley Gomez, and Jim Ziglar. Additionally, I am indebted to Forrest Baty, Rev. Darren Elin, Rev. Cathy George, Ken Halcom, Rev. Stephanie Johnson, and Grace Pomroy for reading early drafts of this material and improving the final product with their thoughtful commentary.

Any errors or misstatements are mine alone.

—James Elrod

# 1 · An Introduction

For I can testify about them that they are zealous for
God, but their zeal is not based on knowledge.

—Romans 10:2

## Nicodemus in the New Millennium

Church leaders in the 2020s may feel a spiritual kinship toward Nicodemus. The Gospel according to John tells us that Nicodemus was a
card-carrying member of the religious establishment of his day. So like
me—and perhaps like you—Nicodemus tried to develop his spiritual
interior in line with the prevailing religious structures. Set aside the centuries, and the situation the Nicodemus of John 3 finds himself in looks
quite familiar.

Nicodemus is intrigued by what he's heard about Jesus and wants
to learn more. Yet he doesn't want to upset the apple cart within his
religious community. Nicodemus proceeds cautiously. He's so anxious
to avoid conflict that he visits Jesus for the first time at night. This noc-
turnal conversation with Jesus evolves into a divine monologue about
judgment and redemption. Nicodemus fails to keep up, but he must
have been impressed.

Nicodemus reappears in John 7 when the chief priests send the
temple police to arrest Jesus. At this critical juncture, Nicodemus inter-
venes, pointing out that the law also guarantees due process. Nicodemus exercises his standing as a leader of his religious community to
alter events. Nicodemus declares that the priests' orders to arrest Jesus
lack authority under the law. Their efforts to arrest Jesus collapse.

John tells us nothing more about Nicodemus in chapter 7. We don't
really know if his spiritual outlook has changed, or if he's simply
offended by the Pharisees' willingness to manipulate Jewish law for

other purposes. We do witness, however, Nicodemus venturing into uncomfortable territory. Nicodemus risks fracturing his personal relationships with his peers to do the right thing. And he does so in a semi-public forum, possibly compromising his own standing within his religious community.

Nicodemus makes his final appearance in John 19. Here Nicodemus assists Joseph of Arimathea in the preparation of Jesus's body for burial. Unlike Joseph, Nicodemus is not described by John as a disciple. Yet his actions speak for themselves. Nicodemus immerses himself in the gritty reality of the day, preparing the body for burial. Nicodemus demonstrates that a vibrant spiritual interior comes with practical consequences. The Nicodemus we met in John 3 has experienced a profound transformation. In John 19 he lives out his faith in spite of the awkwardness it inevitably creates for him within his faith community.

### Money Talk in Church Today

Like Nicodemus in John 3, church leaders generally prefer to avoid conflict. This is particularly true when the conversation centers on the financial status of their church. Two issues make it difficult to have honest conversations about money and church today. Neither have much to do with the threats posed by an increasingly hostile secular culture. First, many churchgoers don't want to hear that you can't have a mission without money. As John Morgan, a pastor with thirty years of congregational experience, says, "We have a cultural problem of talking about money in a religious setting, coming from a tradition that says love of money is the root of all evil."[1] Despite many scriptural precedents to the contrary, calling out the connection between finance and faith makes folks uncomfortable. Because the topic of money is awkward, important conversations about the intersection of money and mission simply don't take place. No wonder Henri Nouwen observed that money conversations are a greater taboo than conversations about sex or religion.[2]

---

1   Quoted in Jim Collins, *Good to Great and the Social Sectors: A Monograph to Accompany Good to Great* (Boulder, CO: Jim Collins, 2005), 18.

2   Henri Nouwen, *A Spirituality of Fundraising* (Nashville, TN: Upper Room Books, 2010), 30.

Clergy often share this reluctance to discuss church money matters openly. In some instances, their hesitancy can be traced to personal misgivings about the proper relationship between wealth and stewardship. Some clergy worry that their willingness to provide pastoral care could be tainted by a detailed understanding of the giving patterns of individual members. So, like their flock, clergy avoid conversations about church finance.

Unless church leaders are willing to discuss the relationship between money and mission openly, they can't build support within the congregation required to create a financially sustainable church. They must internalize—and help their fellow parishioners internalize—the incontrovertible reality that there can be no sustainable mission without a durable financial architecture that supports it.

The second issue is more insidious. New clergy often don't want to engage in money conversations because they don't feel adequately prepared to discuss church financial matters. Few seminaries offer substantive courses in church finance, and fewer still require their students to demonstrate competence in financial matters in order to graduate. For most of the twentieth century, at least in mainline[3] congregations, this formational deficiency didn't have serious repercussions: until the 1990s, clergy could learn the essentials of church finance on the job.

Twentieth-century seminary graduates from mainline traditions typically joined the staff of a financially stable congregation. The average congregation might not be wealthy, but at least it wasn't operating in a perpetual state of financial crisis. Just as important, the typical mainline congregation was served by multiple clergy. Late twentieth-century churches had plenty of mentors for younger staff members. Junior clergy learned how a church functioned through direct observation and practical engagement. They learned by doing. Lessons about church finance were absorbed as they moved up the career ladder. By the time they were called as pastor, senior minister, or head priest, the individual knew a great deal about the inner workings of congregational life, including the essentials of church finance.

---

3  Although the term "mainline" technically refers only to traditional Protestant denominations, in this book the term is intended to apply equally to Black Protestant, Evangelical, and Roman Catholic congregations.

Today few seminary graduates have the opportunity to develop financial skills through a series of postings at financially stable churches. Fewer churches can afford multiple clergy staffs, limiting opportunities for mentorship. Senior clergy have less bandwidth to instruct new clergy on church operations. In the new millennium, organizational stability and deep clergy rosters are the exception rather than the rule. In fact, it is not uncommon for new seminary graduates to be the only professional clergy serving a congregation today. The guild system that helped school clergy on church financial matters still exists, but it no longer functions in a consistent and robust manner. The result is that a large and growing number of today's younger clergy are poorly prepared to handle the financial aspects of congregational life.

It is important to note that this gap in knowledge on the part of new clergy is not a problem of their own making. Seminaries, divinity schools, and denominational offices have not adjusted their curricula or developed new resources to replace the opportunities to learn about church finance on the job that were part of the formation process in the late twentieth century. In mainline denominations, the failure is institutional in nature, not a reflection of the capabilities or commitment of recent seminary graduates. It should surprise no one that the recently ordained are unfamiliar with the fundamentals of church finance; they are products of a system that does little to encourage this aspect of their professional development.

There are also leadership dynamics to consider. Even newly minted clergy are placed on a pedestal by their flock. They are presumed to have an informed view on all church matters, both spiritual and temporal. At a time when the new minister may feel overwhelmed by various demands at the beginning of a call, they may also feel pressure to project competence in financial matters. The new pastor doesn't want to disappoint the congregation right out of the gate. They may also fear that admitting to a lack of financial expertise could have an impact on their job security. The temptation to exaggerate one's grasp of financial matters is not insignificant.

Lay leaders can also feel pressure to wander beyond the natural limits of their own financial expertise. Lay leaders often have meaningful experience in for-profit finance but are not well versed in nonprofit finance. As we will see in chapters 2, 3, and 4, the overlap between for-profit finance and nonprofit finance is significant, but the differences are meaningful. Lay leaders with a financial background sometimes jump in with the best of intentions, only to discover that their frame of reference from the commercial world doesn't translate so well. Honest mistakes are made, mistakes that can impair the congregation's pursuit of its missional goals.

The combined impact of these two issues—the cultural resistance to discussing money matters in church and the limited experience new clergy and lay leaders have with nonprofit finance—means that church leaders lack a shared framework for dealing with their church's financial challenges. They don't share a common vocabulary and they don't agree what best financial practices look like in a church. Consequently, conversations about church money matters can be very frustrating—so frustrating that they are avoided altogether.

## Religion in the New Millennium

For communities of faith, these self-inflicted wounds could not be taking place at a worse time. The first two decades of the twenty-first century have not been kind to organized religion in America. In 2000, when Gallup asked Americans how important religion was in their own lives, 88 percent replied it was very important or fairly important. By 2018, only 73 percent said religion was very important or fairly important. Not surprisingly, the number of Americans who responded that religion was not very important to them rose from 12 percent in 2000 to 26 percent in 2018.[4] Jeffrey Jones of Gallup asserted, "Although the United States is one of the more religious countries, particularly among Western nations, it is far less religious than it used to be."[5]

Pew Research Center, in its landmark 2014 U.S. Religious Landscape Study released in May 2015, came to a similar conclusion. Pew's first religious landscape study took place in 2007 and was based on a nationally representative telephone survey of more than 35,000 Amer-

---

4   https://news.gallup.com/poll/1690/region.aspx.
5   Jeffrey M. Jones, "U.S. Church Membership Down Sharply in Past Two Decades," April 18, 2019, https://news.gallup.com/poll/248837/church-membership-down-sharply-past-two-decades.aspx.

ican adults. The 2014 study was also a telephone survey involving over 35,000 adults. One of the most startling discoveries unearthed by Pew in its 2014 work was that the percentage of adults who identified as religiously unaffiliated, describing themselves as atheist, agnostic, or "nothing in particular," had jumped from 16.1 percent to 22.8 percent in just seven years.[6]

This decline in religiosity was not evenly distributed. As a percentage of the population, adherents to non-Christian faiths (Jewish, Muslim, Buddhist, Hindu, and other world religions) grew about 1 percent. Christianity bore the brunt of shift away from organized religion. The Christian share of the adult U.S. population fell from 78.4 percent to 70.6 percent between 2007 and 2014.

According to Pew, this trend will continue for the foreseeable future. In a separate study released in April 2015, Pew projected a net loss of 28 million Christians in the United States by 2050.[7] Taking into account switching, migration, and population growth, Pew projected Christians would fall from 78 percent to 66 percent of the U.S. population by 2050. This forecast looks conservative. The Christian share had already fallen to 70.6 percent by 2014.

And yet, despite these sobering statistics, the *missio dei* is very much alive in the United States today. Consider the number of congregations. According to sociologist Simon Bauer, the net number of religious congregations in the United States, taking into account both closures and new plantings, has *increased* by approximately 50,000 since the start of the new millennium.[8] There are 50,000 more churches in America today than there were twenty years ago. To paraphrase Mark Twain, reports of the death of religion in America have been greatly exaggerated.

What about the quality of the spiritual life of church members? Pew Research reports that 91 percent of those who were religiously affiliated said religion was either very important or somewhat important in their

---

6   Pew Research Center, "America's Changing Religious Landscape," May 12, 2015, 3, https://www.pewforum.org/2015/05/12/americas-changing-religious-landscape/.

7   Pew Research Center, "The Future of the World's Religions: Population Growth Projections, 2010–2050," April 2, 2015, https://www.pewforum.org/2015/04/02/religious-projections-2010-2050/.

8   Rebecca Randall, "How Many Churches Does America Have? More Than Expected," *Christianity Today,* September 14, 2017, https://www.christianitytoday.com/news/2017/september/how-many-churches-in-america-us-nones-nondenominational.html.

lives in 2014. This was the same result Pew reported when it conducted a similar study in 2007. Among the religiously affiliated, there was also no change in frequency of prayer or service attendance between 2007 and 2014. Those who were seriously engaged with religion in 2007 continued to be seriously engaged in 2014.

Even among Protestants—where the decline in affiliation has been most pronounced—there are signs of life. The loss in membership among Protestant denominations has not been uniformly distributed. Although Evangelical membership declined as a percentage of the total U.S. population, the Southern Baptist Convention, Assemblies of God, Churches of Christ, Lutheran Church-Missouri Synod, and the Presbyterian Church in America collectively added over 2 million members from 2007 to 2014. Historically Black Protestant Churches, such as the National Baptist Convention, Church of God in Christ, African Methodist Episcopal Church, and the Progressive Baptist Convention, collectively enjoyed a constant total membership of approximately 16 million between 2007 and 2014.

Most importantly, individual congregations continue to thrive. Yours may be one of them. Is your church engaging in the kinds of financial practices that assure it will thrive in the years to come? Are your clergy and lay leaders acting as good stewards, adhering to financial practices that lead to missional renewal and growth? When it comes to financial practices, what legacy will current church leadership leave for future generations?

As the Episcopal bishop of Connecticut, Ian Douglas, likes to say, "God's church will continue for centuries. The only question is whether our church will be part of it." The third decade of the New Millennium is not only a moment of transition but also one ripe with opportunity. This book is for clergy, lay leaders, and church members who want to ensure that their congregation will participate in God's once and future church.

### How This Book Can Help

The immediate goal of this book is to facilitate productive conversations about church financial matters among clergy, lay leaders, and church members. It is, by design, brief. It minimizes technical terms and financial jargon whenever possible. The intent is to equip anyone who wants to participate in a discussion on their congregation's financial situation with enough knowledge to do so with confidence. The ultimate goal of this book is to enable committed church leaders to raise their game, empowering congregations to create a financial infrastructure that will support their mission.

Some readers may already know a great deal about the basics of nonprofit accounting and finance. They are less interested in learning about the fundamentals of church finance and more interested in recent changes in the environment that impact their church's financial outlook. For example, they might be more interested in learning about what's new in the fundraising world than why earning an operating surplus is crucial for any church. The book is structured with the needs of different audiences in mind. Each chapter is self-contained and can be read separately.

You may find reading the book with a group of colleagues is helpful. Having an opportunity to discuss this material with your peers will reinforce new concepts. Group discussion can be particularly useful if you decide some of the concepts might be applicable to your situation.

This book is not another treatise on the decline of traditional religious practices and the dangers that accompany rising secularism. Nor is it a cookbook with recipes guaranteed to improve a church's financial position. It is, instead, a primer designed to facilitate productive conversations among clergy and lay leaders about the financial challenges their church is facing. Unless church leaders find a way to overcome their congregation's reluctance to talk about money, the mission of their church will eventually be jeopardized. Money makes God's work possible on earth. In the final analysis, this is really a book about creating, preserving, and growing God's church.

## Questions to Consider

1. Does your church regularly provide financial information to the congregation in a transparent, understandable format?

2. Do you have the background and experience to discuss your church's financial position with confidence?

3. Are you comfortable discussing your congregation's financial challenges with other church members?"

# 2 · Terminologies and Typologies

> I also told them about the gracious hand of my God
> on me and what the king had said to me. They re-
> plied, "Let us start rebuilding." So they began this
> good work.
>
> —Nehemiah 2:18

## Tower of Babel II

When church leaders first dig into church financial matters, they sometimes feel they've entered a modern-day Tower of Babel. They confront
new terms, some of which strike them as duplicative if not contradicto-
ry. They encounter financial statements that resemble ones they've seen
in the commercial world, but these reports are designed for other purposes. They even hear terms they thought they knew but are now used
in different ways. Their enthusiasm to wade into the financial aspects of
church life starts to ebb before it can flow.

The skies grow darker if they ask for information on the financial
results of other churches. Surely there must be evidence on best financial practices in churches so the congregation can set some goals.
Unfortunately, comparable financial information rarely exists. Without
an independent frame of reference, church leaders find themselves in
the situation described by Dale Berra, son of baseball great Yogi Berra,
on a family trip to the Baseball Hall of Fame. Yogi had no map. When
Berra's wife said, "Yogi, you're lost," he replied, "Yes, but we're making
great time."[1]

---

1 Marc Myers, "A Perfect Game Inspired Dale Berra's First Name," *The Wall Street
Journal,* May 12, 2020, https://www.wsj.com/articles/a-perfect-game-inspired-dale-berras-
first-name-11589288739.

## A Structural Trinity

Churches are organizations that are simultaneously charitable, non-profit, and tax-exempt. What do the terms "charitable," "nonprofit," and "tax-exempt" actually mean, and how do we understand them in relation to a church? Charities, organizations that serve the less fortunate, have existed in Western Europe since the late Middle Ages and in North America since colonial times. Churches have historically helped the poor, infirm, and destitute, and as a result, they are classified in the organizational typology of the federal government as charitable organizations.

Because the federal government presumes all churches are inherently charitable, churches are also presumed to meet the Internal Revenue Service (IRS) criteria to qualify as tax-exempt organizations. Federal tax exemption confers a number of economic benefits. Tax-exempt organizations are entities not required to pay federal income tax on profits generated from their operations. Because most state and local governments that impose an income tax follow the federal precedent, tax-exempt organizations receive additional economic benefits in those states by virtue of this federal characterization. Finally, based on their tax-exempt classification, many tax-exempt organizations receive relief from franchise and real estate taxes by state and local governments.

It's worth repeating that churches don't need to be designated as tax-exempt by the IRS; they are tax-exempt in the eyes of the federal government by virtue of their presumed charitability. Every other kind of organization that wants to become tax-exempt and receive the associated economic benefits must submit a formal application to the Internal Revenue Service. If their application is approved, they must agree to comply with a variety on ongoing reporting requirements. Chief among these is the filing of Form 990[2] on an annual basis. Form 990 requires detailed financial and operational information, including the compensation of senior employees. Churches do not have to file Form 990 or comply with other reporting requirements.

---

2   A number of different versions of Form 990 have been created by the IRS over time and now include Form 990-EZ, Form 990-N, Form 990-PF, and Form 990-T. See www.irs.gov.

Unlike other tax-exempt organizations, churches receive the benefits of tax exemption without incurring the costs associated with ongoing reporting.

Finally, churches are nonprofit organizations. There is considerable confusion surrounding the term "nonprofit organization." Even the self-proclaimed largest network of nonprofit organizations in the United States—The Council of Nonprofits—does not seem to know what the term means.[3] Like Justice Potter Stewart, who famously wrestled with the definition of pornography in *Jacobellis v. Ohio*, most folks think they will know a nonprofit organization when they see one.

Fortunately, there is consensus regarding the distinguishing characteristics of nonprofit organizations. The two common attributes of all nonprofit organizations are that they do not have owners and their primary purpose is not to generate a profit. This does not mean nonprofits lack stakeholders, or that they are prohibited from making a profit. It does mean that the rules which govern the commercial world don't always apply in the nonprofit world. A good working definition of a nonprofit organization is an enterprise whose activities benefit society at large by addressing the needs of specific populations and where generating a profit is not the primary motivation.

All nonprofit organizations, including churches, utilize the same accounting principles. The same conventions the accounting profession has adopted for universities, museums, and social service organizations also apply to churches. It is therefore no surprise that the format of a church's audited financial statements looks very much like the format of the audited financial statements of the local hospital or Red Cross.

The financial record-keeping for nonprofit organizations, including churches, is based on the principles of fund accounting. (Fund accounting is described in more detail in chapter 3.) The structure of fund accounting is quite different from that of for-profit accounting, where the chief concern is to determine whether the firm made a profit. Fund accounting is designed to make sure that any donated funds the organization receives that come with restrictions are used according to

---

3   https://www.councilofnonprofits.org/what-is-a-nonprofit.

the wishes of the donor. The way a church reports its financial results is therefore different from the way a commercial enterprise reports its financial results.

In summary, the federal government concluded that because churches perform charitable acts, they should be classified as charitable organizations. This presumption of inherent charitability automatically rendered all churches, in the eyes of the government, as tax-exempt. Unlike other tax-exempt organizations, churches have no ongoing reporting requirements to the IRS. (It is pointless to monitor their activities because the IRS can't revoke their tax-exempt status.) Finally, churches are nonprofit organizations. They conduct their affairs absent a primary focus on making a profit. Consequently, churches are subject to the same accounting conventions that dictate how other nonprofit organizations report their financial results. The financial profile of every church is a function of its tripartite status as a charitable, tax-exempt, and nonprofit organization.

## A Rose by Any Other Name

It's not uncommon for business-savvy church leaders to find church finance hopelessly confusing when they first get involved. Anyone with a background in for-profit finance comes to church finance from a profit-making perspective. They expect to receive a set of audited financial statements that includes an income statement, a balance sheet, and a cash flow statement. These statements are designed to let the reader know if the organization is creating economic value for its shareholders. Things, they discover, are different in church.

First, the titles of the financial reports are different. The income statement is called an operating statement, an activity statement, a statement of revenues, expenses, and changes in fund balance, a statement of changes in net assets, or a statement of activities and changes in net assets. The balance sheet is called a statement of financial position, a statement of assets and net assets, or a statement of assets and liabilities and fund balances. Fluidity in titles is distracting but hardly insurmountable; most financially astute readers get their bearings in short order.[4]

---

4   This text uses the terms "statement of activities," "statement of financial position," "statement of cash flows," and "statement of functional expenses" throughout.

Within each report, however, certain line-item entries can cause genuine confusion. The most problematic of these is the church's bottom line. At first glance, there doesn't appear to be a bottom line in the financial reports of most churches.

Perhaps because church members have such difficulty in talking about money, the net income of a church is rarely labeled net income. It is called something (anything!) else, such as surplus, operating income, operating surplus, excess of revenues over expenses, or change in net assets. Talking about financial sustainability is difficult when the organization, with the assent of the accounting profession, assiduously avoids mentioning profitability. Net income, like the name of Lord Voldemort in J. K. Rowling's Harry Potter series, must never be mentioned.

Another potential source of confusion for church newcomers is a financial report that does not appear in the audited financial statements of for-profit organizations. This is the statement of functional expenses. This report describes, in a matrix format, two years of expenses found in the statement of activities in great detail. The expenses are allocated according to program categories or support services. The statement of functional expenses is not confusing on its surface, but it does not explain what is in each category or the allocation methodology it employs for indirect expenses. Without a firm understanding of the underlying assumptions, the statement of functional expenses can raise misplaced concerns about expense management in a church.

These and other differences in the financial statements of nonprofit and for-profit organizations can cloud conversations on church finance. The differences are not arbitrary, however. The orientation of nonprofit and for-profit organizations are fundamentally different, and the composition of their financial statements reflects this difference in orientation. Regina Herzlinger and Denise Nitterhouse illuminate this issue in their description of the statement of activities (operating statement) of a nonprofit organization:

> The difference between for-profit and nonprofit Operating Statement titles is more than symbolic. It reflects the nonprofit organizations' focus on the flows of financial resources, rather than net income. The primary objective of nonprofit organiza-

tions is to provide services, not to earn a profit. Financial operations support and enhance their ability to provide services by balancing sources and uses of financial resources. Nonprofits must manage their financial operations prudently to ensure that they own financial resources adequate for continued service provision. For them, financial success should not be an end in itself.[5]

Chapter 3 will describe the form and function of church financial statements in more detail.

Herzlinger and Nitterhouse's observation highlights the insoluble bond between a church's mission and its financial infrastructure. Mission is always the primary consideration. Church leaders must make sure that the financial resources required by the mission flow to it without interruption. Financial structure plays an essential role in the mission by enabling the mission to continue unabated.

## Entering the Fourth Dimension

For most of the twentieth century, the organizational composition of most churches looked like the organizational composition of most secular social services organizations: charitable, tax-exempt, and nonprofit. Churches weren't required to report their financial results to the IRS, and therefore operated with greater confidentiality.[6] Secular nonprofits had to report their financial results but, from a practical perspective, those reports were not accessible by the public. All nonprofits, not only churches, operated without a great deal of financial transparency. Changes in IRS collection and reporting practices altered the landscape for secular social services firms. These changes did not apply to churches directly. Because virtually all other tax-exempt organizations became more financially transparent while churches did not, these changes brought with them new challenges for religious institutions.

---

5   Regina E. Herzlinger and Denise Nitterhouse, *Financial Accounting and Managerial Control for Nonprofit Organizations* (Cincinnati, OH: South-Western Publishing Co., 1994), 96–97.

6   Denominational control and reporting standards established by the accounting profession imposed practical limitations on congregational agency when it came to financial practices.

The IRS began collecting financial information from tax-exempt organizations on Form 990 in 1941. As long as the information collected by the IRS was collected and stored on paper or microfiche cards in Washington, DC, it was largely inaccessible to anyone outside the federal government. This situation changed dramatically with the adoption of electronic submission of Form 990 by the IRS.[7] By 2011, the IRS estimated that 60 percent of all tax filings were submitted electronically. In 2016, the IRS began releasing submitted Form 990s to the public in a machine-readable format. This digital revolution reached fruition with enactment of The Taxpayer First Act of 2019 (HR 3151). Among other things, The Taxpayer First Act required that every organization submitting Form 990 must do so electronically for all fiscal years after July 1, 2019. Beginning in 2021, anyone with access to the internet can download the operating and financial information on every tax-exempt organization required to file with the IRS instantaneously at virtually no cost.

The emergence of a comprehensive, searchable database on the financial results of secular social services organizations means they have developed a fourth distinguishing characteristic: charitable, nonprofit, tax-exempt organizations that file Form 990 have also become *searchable* organizations. Their results will receive increased scrutiny because interested parties can access information on them with ease. Their results can be compared on an apples-to-apples basis with similar organizations. Best practices can be identified and theories on performance can be tested for statistical significance. Searchable organizations will be searched because they can be searched. Churches are not searchable in this way and can only watch as the searchable parade gains momentum.[8]

---

7    The IRS launched a pilot program for electronic filing in 1986. It was not until 1998 when Congress mandated a goal of 80 percent e-file rate for all federal tax returns that electronic filing became ubiquitous. For a more complete history of e-filing, see https://www.irs.gov/pub/irs-news/fs-11-10.pdf.

8    Churches can become more searchable by curating a digital presence that includes Form 990 style information. Third-party organizations, such as the Evangelical Council for Financial Accountability and MinistryWatch, publish financial and operating information on churches. Denominations collect and distribute financial and operating information on their affiliates on a selective basis. But no comprehensive database on church performance can be queried by an interested third party easily and without cost. Churches are not, by IRS standards, searchable organizations.

The emergence of the searchable organization has two potentially serious implications for churches. First, academic and other third-party interest in searchable organizations will increase. Third-party interest in religious organizations—not a priority in academic circles for many years—will decrease. Operating and financial results for searchable organizations can be analyzed on the basis of robust, comparative information. The results for churches can't be observed and compared. Unlike leaders of secular nonprofit organizations, church leaders can't arm themselves with objective information needed to change behavior and improve results.

Second, donors will expect to receive more operating and financial information from the tax-exempt organizations they support. As described in chapters 6 and 7, tax-exempt organizations rely on a shrinking number of donors for support, and the ways those donors want to engage in philanthropy are changing. In the twentieth century, churches typically appealed to their members for financial support on the basis of loyalty and scripture. This may no longer be sufficient.

Donors want to see how their gifts make a difference. Searchable organizations have trained donors to demand evidence their gifts are making a difference by leaning in and providing information on relative performance. In a searchable world, it's best to take control of the narrative rather than eliminate risk ceding control or misinterpretation. Churches, unlike searchable organizations, can't easily compile and present this kind of information. The inability to do so makes them look increasingly out of step with the rest of the charitable universe.

## Summary

The financial information a church produces and presents is a reflection of its charitable, tax-exempt, and nonprofit character. In chapter 3, we'll examine a set of church financial statements and discover some of the implications of this character. Because the goal of nonprofit (fund) accounting is fundamentally different from for-profit (corporate) accounting, church leaders with a corporate financial background find it takes some adjustment to apply their experience in a church context.

Recent changes in the availability of financial and operating information on secular tax-exempt organizations threaten churches indirectly. Churches, relative to these searchable organizations, are more difficult to research. This makes it difficult to compare the results of a church with other secular and religious organizations. If church donors become accustomed to receiving more detailed financial and operating information from the secular nonprofits they support—particularly information on comparative performance—the ability of a church to grow its revenues could be compromised.

## Questions to Consider

1. Does the membership of your church see a connection between financial sustainability and mission? How do you know?

2. Are your church leaders financially literate when it comes to nonprofit financial matters?

3. Do you believe donor engagement with other nonprofit organizations influences the amount they give to their church, or is giving to a church "just different"?

# 3 · Church Financial Statements

Consider now, for the Lord has chosen you to build
a house as the sanctuary. Be strong and do the work.

—1 Chronicles 28:10

## Concepts and Counting

What's the first thing that springs to mind when a clergyperson receives a call to lead a congregation? Or when a lay leader is asked to
take a seat on the governing board of their church? Accounting principles, financial reporting, and endowments? Probably not. Yet clergy
and lay leaders eventually discover that a congregation's mission and
money issues can't be separated. We'll review this interrelationship in
more detail in chapter 9. Clergy and lay leaders may also discover that
it's difficult to oversee the affairs of their congregation effectively without a grasp of certain fundamental financial concepts that affect their
church's mission.

The mechanics of good financial management are complex, and even
a rudimentary explanation would transcend the scope of this book.
There are plenty of resources available for anyone who wants to learn
more about the intricacies of nonprofit accounting and finance. You
don't need to become a financial expert to play a constructive role in
the financial management of your church. You need, instead, to become
familiar with a few overarching concepts and the basic structure of a
church's financial statements. Neither these concepts nor the financial
statements are difficult to understand. Once you understand them,
you'll be able to answer important questions about church finance
including: Who determines the financial practices of my church? What
principles inform financial record-keeping at my church? What kind of
financial reports does my church produce, and why? And what is the

most critical aspect of my church's financial condition I should always keep in mind?

### Concept 1: Church Leadership Has Responsibility for All Financial Practices

This first concept may strike you as self-evident. It is, however, fundamental to everything that follows, so it deserves exploration: church leadership, and only church leadership, has responsibility for the financial practices of their church. Some church leaders, particularly those without a background in nonprofit finance or law, assume that third parties, such the Internal Revenue Service, the Securities and Exchange Commission, or the Financial Accounting Standards Board (FASB) impose financial practices from on high. If regulatory bodies and trade groups don't dictate financial practices, they assume the church's independent auditors, the financial staff, or in mainline congregations, the denominational hierarchy makes these decisions. Naïve church leaders envision themselves as docile bystanders, charged with implementing policies and procedures fashioned by someone else.

In fact, church leaders choose what financial practices their church will maintain. Church leaders have agency when it comes to financial practices, just as they do in the other aspects of congregational life. This agency, and the responsibility that comes with it, is rarely discussed. Not because the topic is intentionally suppressed, or because it doesn't merit thoughtful review, but because questions about the appropriateness of a church's financial practices don't surface very often. Why not?

One reason is that most clergy and lay volunteers aren't particularly eager to delve into their church's financial practices and so they don't raise the question. We discussed in chapter 1 the cultural prejudices against talking about money in church. Church leaders would rather spend their time on congregational life and matters of faith. Or they feel they simply don't have the time. Some combination of scripture, doctrine, music, liturgy, ritual, evangelism, community, and outreach brought them to this church. They didn't join church so they could help run a small nonprofit business. They don't really want to spend time on boiler room issues like financial policy. And so, absent a crisis, they don't.

There's another reason that church leaders avoid discussing financial practices. Creating and implementing new financial practices is painful and expensive. Staff and volunteers, who may have been doing things the same way for years, find change threatening or uncomfortable (or both) and resist. Changing existing financial procedures invariably requires additional staff time and often requires additional funding. Financial practice is a can that can be kicked down the road without immediate negative consequences. Intentionally and unintentionally, church leaders elect to do just that. Kick as they might, the responsibility for the financial well-being of their church still rests squarely on their shoulders.

## Concept 2: A Decision Not to Change Is Still a Decision

Every time church leaders pass a resolution to accept the report on the audited financial statements from the church's auditors, authorize a financial summary for distribution at the annual meeting, or endorse the submission of a financial report to denominational hierarchy, they are reaffirming an existing financial practice. Rarely do church leaders stop and ask whether these reports should continue to be issued in their current form, or whether they should be issued at all. If these financial practices are still relevant, should they be modified? Are the church's current financial practices the best available financial practices, or the consequence of full calendars, inattention, and church politics? Do the form, frequency, and content of these reports meet the current needs of the congregation? Maintaining existing financial practices is a passive form of decision-making, but it is a form of decision-making nonetheless.

Most financial decision-making in churches takes place passively. Too often financial decisions are made through the unexamined affirmation of existing financial policies and practices that someone else thought made sense at the time. Defaulting to past practice, however, doesn't absolve church leadership from its fiduciary responsibilities. The activities surrounding financial decision-making in a church can be delegated; responsibility for the consequences of those decisions cannot.

## Concept 3: Don't Spend Time on Financial Policies You Can't Really Influence

Let's assume, as a church leader, you understand that you are responsible for the financial practices of your church. You want to become more conversant in financial matters and not just rubber-stamp current practice without thoughtful review. How can you spend your time most effectively in your efforts to become better informed about church financial matters?

One way to begin is to separate church financial policies into two broad categories: financial policies that, in light of practical considerations, you are unlikely to change; and financial policies, in light of practical considerations, you can influence. Your responsibility for your church's financial practices, of course, remains unaffected, but in terms of using your time wisely, you'll benefit by distinguishing between those financial practices where your efforts are unlikely to change behavior from those where they might.

Church leaders have no effective agency when it comes to bookkeeping, fund accounting, and standard financial reporting (assuming the church wants to adhere to generally accepted accounting principles so it can receive a "clean" opinion letter from its auditors). Bookkeeping is the process of recording financial transactions. The mechanics of good bookkeeping are the same in all business settings, for-profit and nonprofit alike. Each economic transaction is recorded in a book called a ledger.[1] The ledger is organized into separate accounts, categorized according to whether the transaction affects revenues, expenses, assets, or liabilities.

Every transaction is entered in two accounts, which is why bookkeeping is sometimes referred to as double-entry bookkeeping. Every time the organization incurs an expense, the organization's resources for meeting that expense are reduced. Because every transaction is entered twice, double-entry bookkeeping provides a system of checks and balances that helps avoid errors. Periodically, results are totaled up and summarized. Double-entry bookkeeping has stood the test of time:

---

1   Today bookkeeping often takes place through software rather than a physical ledger. The application of bookkeeping principles is agnostic to the medium.

it hasn't changed meaningfully since it was developed in medieval Italy during the Middle Ages.[2]

Like bookkeeping, fund accounting is a financial practice where church leaders have no effective agency. Church bookkeeping is organized according to the principles of fund accounting. Fund accounting, at its core, is chiefly concerned with the proper treatment of donated assets. Sometimes nonprofit organizations receive donations that can be spent for any lawful purpose. However, nonprofit organizations also receive gifts that come with restrictions.

Nonprofit organizations have a legal obligation to keep track of where and when the money is spent if a donor specifies how a gift must be used. If donors never specified how or when their gifts could be spent, there would be no need for fund accounting. Fund accounting is designed to make sure that the wishes of donors who stipulate how their gifts are used will be honored.

Regina Herzlinger and Denise Nitterhouse offer this helpful analogy for anyone interested in how fund accounting works:

> To satisfy this stewardship purpose, accounting entries are classified by *funds*. Each fund is like a cookie jar in which resources restricted for different purposes are stored. A fund is a separate accounting entity that records the sources and uses of the resources it contains. Funds are separated from each other because their resources are restricted to certain specific purposes. The quantity of resources in each fund and its sources and uses are accounted for in the process called *fund accounting*.[3]

Standard financial reporting for a church is the final area of financial policy where church leadership has no effective agency. Nonprofit organizations that subscribe to generally accepted accounting principles produce four basic financial reports:

---

2 Church leaders must, of course, make sure that the church's books are kept honestly. The point here is that church leaders are unlikely to influence the mechanics of bookkeeping.

3 Regina E. Herzlinger and Denise Nitterhouse, *Financial Accounting and Managerial Control for Nonprofit Organizations* (Cincinnati, OH: South-Western Publishing, 1994), 186.

A *Statement of Financial Position*, which is the equivalent of a balance sheet in the for-profit world. The Statement of Financial Position lists the assets (what the church owns), liabilities (what the church owes), and net assets (what the church owns less what the church owes) of the church at a point in time, typically the end of a fiscal year.

A *Statement of Activities*, which is the equivalent of an income statement in the for-profit world. The Statement of Activities records revenue coming in and expenses going out of the organization during a period of time, typically one fiscal year.

A *Statement of Cash Flows*, which is similar to the statement of cash flows in the for-profit world. The Statement of Cash Flows shows the flow of cash receipts into, and cash payments out of, the church's accounts. The Statement of Cash Flows reports how much cash the organization had at the beginning and end of a period in time, typically one fiscal year.

A *Statement of Functional Expenses*, which has no analog in the for-profit world. The Statement of Functional Expenses categorizes expenses by function (program, management and general, and fundraising) and by type of expense (salaries, benefits, etc.). The Statement of Functional Expenses provides details on where money was spent during a period of time, typically one fiscal year.

Each of these reports is a financial statement in its own right. When grouped together, these four statements are commonly referred to as *the* financial statements of the church.

Church leadership, to be clear, has agency over all financial practices, including bookkeeping, fund accounting, and standard financial statements. It generally chooses not to exercise its agency in these matters. The issue is not whether their agency exists, but whether the church would be better off if church leadership decided the church should veer away from these bedrock financial practices.

The downside of diversion is easily imagined. Not complying with generally accepted accounting principles would make it impossible to receive a clean opinion from the church's auditors. Banks often condition the extension of credit upon the receipt of a clean audit opinion. The church's financial results would no longer be comparable with the results of other churches in the area or the denomination. Bad publicity might follow if an independent evaluator, such as MinistryWatch, learned of the change and characterized it as a negative development. Consequently, few church leaders seriously consider deviating from these elemental financial conventions.

### Concept 4: Spend Time on Financial Practices You Really Can Influence

Church leaders can spend their time productively and exercise genuine agency by focusing on the potential opportunities created by supplementary financial reporting. This may involve repurposing existing content, creating new content, and distributing content through new channels. In every case, supplementary financial reporting involves revealing information the church is not compelled to reveal, but chooses to do so. It does so because church leaders believe the information serves the needs and interests of church stakeholders, and thereby supports the mission of the congregation.

Churches that retain five years of budgets and audited financial statements have an inventory of existing content that can be repurposed. For example, focusing exclusively in a budget meeting on the church's current financial results and how they compare with next year's budget only tells part of the story. How good is the church at projecting revenue and expense, based on five years of budgets and actual results? How does that track record inform the assumptions behind the proposed budget? What was the respective compound annual growth rate of revenues and expenses over the past five years? Did one-time financial events, positive or negative, materially influence the church's ability to meet its projections? Is the church spending more or less on administration and overhead than it did five years ago? Should the answers to these questions be distributed before the meeting so all of the participants have a common frame of reference before the conversation begins?

Church leaders can also call for the creation of new content that highlights the church's efforts to realize its mission. For example, should the annual meeting quantify—not just describe in glowing terms—the congregation's progress toward realizing its mission over the past year? Has the church dedicated an increasing percentage of its revenues to community outreach, and if so, have the funds been used to fortify existing programs or expand into new areas? Did the average annual donation by giving unit increase, tangible evidence of the congregation's support for the mission? How did actual results compare to the church's goals at the start of the year?

Distributing content through new channels is generally the most valuable—and the most controversial—aspect of supplementary financial reporting. Consider, for example, the potential benefits of putting the church's most recent audited financial statements on its website. The financial statements already exist, so there is no additional cost. Members interested in the church's financial position could do their own research, saving staff time and the cost of printing and sending hard copies. In a fundraising environment that leans toward greater transparency, as described in chapters 6 and 7, making financial results available might encourage greater generosity. Yet the National Study of Congregations' Economic Practices discovered that only 5 percent of the churches it surveyed in 2017 posted financial information on their website.[4]

Distribution of content—rather than the repurposing or creation of content—can provoke intense debates within a congregation. If members are uncomfortable talking about money and mission among themselves, imagine the anxiety about revealing what the congregation does with its money to the outside world! The distribution of financial information taps into a deeper reservoir of angst: it forces members to come to terms with their personal conception of stewardship.

Are we revealing information about *our* assets or *God's* assets? If a church's assets are the province of the membership, the principles of confidentiality that members exercise in their personal affairs is a reasonable approach. If a church's assets are the province of God, principles of inclusion, transparency, and evangelism should serve as

---

4   David P. King, Christopher W. Munn, Brad R. Fulton, and Jamie L. Goodwin, "The National Study of Congregations' Economic Practices," NSCEP, September 16, 2019, 23, https://www.nscep.org/wp-content/uploads/2019/09/Lake_NSCEP_09162019-F-LR.pdf.

True North. Gerald Kuecher distills the many biblical precedents on stewardship in one short sentence: "Stewardship is the understanding that we are not owners; we hold God's gifts in trust."[5] Decisions concerning what financial information to share and how to share it are ultimately governed by the congregation's collective understanding of stewardship.

## Reading Church Financial Statements

These four concepts—church leaders are responsible for their church's financial practices; perpetuating existing financial practices is a decision; don't spend time on financial matters you can't influence; and do spend time on financial matters you can influence—merely set the table. At some point, clergy and lay leaders must roll up their sleeves and engage directly with the church's financial statements. Exhibits 3-1, 3-2, 3-3, 3-4, and 3-5 are the audited financial statements of a congregation known as Any Church. These exhibits demonstrate the purpose of each document and how these documents relate to one another.

Exhibit 3-1

**Any Church · Statement of Financial Position**
(*$ in thousands*)

|  | Dec. 31, 2018 | Dec. 31, 2019 | Dec. 31, 2020 |
|---|---|---|---|
| Assets |  |  |  |
| Cash & Equivalents | $ 1,082 | $ 615 | $ 219 |
| Investments | $ 3,071 | $ 3,508 | $ 3,906 |
| Property & Equipment (Net) | $ 1,399 | $ 1,317 | $ 1,299 |
| **Total Assets** | **$ 5,552** | **$ 5,440** | **$ 5,424** |
| Liabilities | 4 | 4 | 3 |
| Net Assets |  |  |  |
| Net Assets without Donor Restriction | $ 1,849 | 0 | 0 |
| Net Assets with Donor Restrictions | $ 3,699 | 0 | 0 |
| **Total Net Assets** | **$ 5,548** | **$ 5,436** | **$ 5,421** |
| **Total Liabilities and Net Assets** | **$ 5,552** | **$ 5,440** | **$ 5,424** |

---

5 Gerald W. Keucher, *Remember the Future: Financial Leadership and Asset Management for Congregations* (New York: Church Publishing, 2006), 148.

The Statement of Financial Position (Exhibit 3-1) provides a snapshot of Any Church's financial situation for three years at the end of the calendar year 2020. It lists the resources the church has acquired to support its mission (assets) and where those assets came from (liabilities plus net assets). Chapter 4 describes some of the challenges Any Church has encountered in financing its mission. Unlike the other three financial reports, which are concerned with the movement of resources over time, the Statement of Financial Position reflects Any Church's financial situation at a specific point in time (December 31, the end of each fiscal year).

The distinguishing characteristic of Any Church's Statement of Financial Position is that it "balances" (which is why it is called a balance sheet in the for-profit world). Total assets on the top of the page *always* equals the sum of liabilities (amounts owed) plus net assets (total of annual surpluses and deficits generated by the organization since it was formed). As of December 31, 2020, Any Church had collected $5,424,000 in assets to pursue its mission. It financed these resources through $3,000 of borrowings and $5,421,000 of net assets, sometimes called accumulated surpluses.

In the for-profit world, net assets are called shareholders' equity, because the value of the organization is the property of its shareholders (owners). If the organization was liquidated, once all debts were paid off, the residual value would be the property of its shareholders. Since no one owns Any Church, the residual value of the enterprise is labeled total net assets. The residual value belongs to the organization (understood as the denomination in some instances and the individual congregation in others, depending on polity) rather than its members. Note that in deference to the principles of fund accounting, these total net assets are broken down into those with and without donor restrictions.

The Statement of Activities (Exhibit 3-2) shows how financial resources flow in and out of Any Church over a period of time. In the case of Any Church, $1,304,000 of total revenue came into the church from January 1, 2020, to December 31, 2020. Any Church spent $1,102,000 providing services and programs, generating a surplus of $202,000 from operations, labeled by Any Church as a change in net assets from operations.

Exhibit 3-2

**Any Church · Statement of Activities**
(*$ in thousands*)

| | Dec. 31, 2019 | Dec. 31, 2020 |
|---|---|---|
| Revenue | | |
| Contributions | $ 806 | $ 777 |
| Bequests | 0 | $ 450 |
| Other | $ 122 | $ 77 |
| **Total Revenue** | $ 928 | $ 1,304 |
| Expenses | | |
| Program Services | $ 649 | $ 655 |
| Management & General | $ 440 | $ 447 |
| **Total Expenses** | $ 1,089 | $ 1,102 |
| Change in Net Assets from Operations | (161) | 202 |
| Non-Operating Items | | |
| Realized Gains (Losses) on Investments | $ 37 | $ 34 |
| Unrealized Gains (Losses) on Investments | $ 12 | (225) |
| Loss on Sale of Property & Equipment | 0 | (26) |
| **Change in Net Assets** | $ (112) | $ (15) |
| Net Assets | | |
| Beginning of Year | $ 5,548 | $ 5,436 |
| End of Year | $ 5,436 | $ 5,421 |

Any Church also has a significant investment portfolio that supports its mission. The Statement of Financial Position (Exhibit 3-1) indicates these assets totaled $3,906,000 at the end of 2020. The performance of Any Church's investment portfolio, along with other nonoperating items, is netted against the $202,000 surplus from operations. Apparently, 2020 was not a banner year for investment management at Any Church. Any Church exited 2020 with $15,000 fewer net assets than it held at the beginning of the year. The sum total of economic activity at Any Church in 2020 is reflected on the Statement of Financial Position, which shows that total net assets declined from $5,436,000 on December 31, 2019 to $5,421,000 on December 31, 2020—a difference of

$15,000. (This same $15,000 change in net assets appears at the bottom of the Statement of Activities.)

It should be clear that the Statement of Activities has an active dialogue with the Statement of Financial Position. The operating and nonoperating financial results from running the church for a year are summarized in the Statement of Activities and reflected on a certain date in the Statement of Financial Position. Whether the results are positive or negative, they affect the residual value of the enterprise. In the case of Any Church, the organization has suffered a modest $15,000 decline in value between the end of 2019 and the end of 2020.

Exhibit 3-3

| Any Church · Statement of Cash Flows ($ in thousands) | Dec. 31, 2019 | Dec. 31, 2020 |
|---|---|---|
| **Cash Flow from Operating Activities** | | |
| Change in Net Assets | $ (112) | $ (15) |
| Adjustments for Noncash and Working Capital Items: | | |
| Depreciation | $ 110 | $ 103 |
| Loss on Sale of Property & Equipment | $ 0 | $ 26 |
| Realized (Gains) Losses on investments | $ (37) | $ (34) |
| Unrealized (Gains) Losses on Investments | $ (12) | $ 225 |
| Change in Employee Witholdings Payable | $ 0 | $ (1) |
| **Net Cash from Operating Activities** | $ (51) | $ 304 |
| **Cash Flow from Investing Activities** | | |
| Purchase of Investments | $ (539) | $ (670) |
| Proceeds from Sale of Investments | $ 151 | $ 81 |
| Purchase of Property & Equipment | $ (28) | $ (132) |
| Proceeds from Sale of Property & Equipment | $ 0 | $ 21 |
| Net Cash from Investing Activities | $ (416) | $ (700) |
| **Net Change in Cash and Equivalents** | $ (467) | $ (396) |
| **Cash and Equivalents** | | |
| Beginning of Year | $ 1,082 | $ 615 |
| End of Year | $ 615 | $ 219 |

The Statement of Cash Flows (Exhibit 3-3) focuses on the movement of one kind of financial asset—cash—in and out of Any Church during 2020. Thomas Ittleson says, "The Statement of Cash Flows is just like your checkbook register. You subtract an amount when you spend money and add an amount when you deposit money. . . . The Statement of Cash Flows summarizes the organization's payments (cash outflows) and deposits (cash inflows) for a period of time."[6] Like the Statement of Activities (Exhibit 3-2), the Statement of Cash Flows reflects how the results of Any Church during 2020 impacted its cash position on December 31, 2020.

Also like the Statement of Activities, the Statement of Cash Flows has an active dialogue with the Statement of Financial Position. On the bottom of Exhibit 3-3, we find that Any Church began 2020 with $615,000 in cash. This is the same amount that Any Church had on hand the last day of 2019 in Exhibit 3-1 (see the center column). The Statement of Cash Flows details how operating and investment activities affected the cash position of the church. Note that the very first item in Exhibit 3-3 is the $15,000 loss for 2020 that appeared in both the Statement of Financial Position (reflected as a decline in total net assets between 2019 and 2020) and the Statement of Activities (reflected as the change in net assets), making the Statement of Cash Flows the most interactive of the financial reports we've reviewed.

---

6  Thomas R. Ittleson, *Nonprofit Accounting & Financial Statements: Overview for Board, Management, and Staff,* rev. 2nd ed. (Cambridge: Mercury Group Press, 2017), 59.

Exhibit 3-4

**Any Church · Statement of Functional Expenses**
(*$ in thousands*)

| | For the Year Ended Dec. 31, 2019 | | | | | |
| | Worship | Outreach | Music | Total Program | Management & General | Total Expenses |
|---|---|---|---|---|---|---|
| Compensation | $ 109 | $ 27 | $ 180 | $ 316 | $ 87 | $ 403 |
| Housing | 14 | 3 | 0 | 17 | 2 | 19 |
| Benefits | 54 | 15 | 2 | 71 | 16 | 87 |
| Depreciation | 38 | 2 | 0 | 40 | 70 | 110 |
| Utilities | 22 | 3 | 0 | 25 | 57 | 82 |
| Insurance | 4 | 0 | 0 | 4 | 11 | 15 |
| Worship | 91 | 0 | 49 | 140 | 0 | 140 |
| Education | 18 | 0 | 0 | 18 | 0 | 18 |
| Professional Fees | 0 | 0 | 0 | 0 | 24 | 24 |
| Communications | 0 | 0 | 0 | 0 | 17 | 17 |
| Other | 16 | 2 | 0 | 18 | 156 | 174 |
| Total Expenses | $ 366 | $ 52 | $ 231 | $ 649 | $ 440 | $ 1,089 |

Exhibit 3-5

**Any Church · Statement of Functional Expenses**
(*$ in thousands*)

| | For the Year Ended Dec. 31, 2020 | | | | | |
| | Worship | Outreach | Music | Total Program | Management & General | Total Expenses |
|---|---|---|---|---|---|---|
| Compensation | $ 119 | $ 29 | $ 183 | $ 331 | $ 88 | $ 419 |
| Housing | 16 | 3 | 0 | 19 | 2 | 21 |
| Benefits | 46 | 13 | 32 | 91 | 15 | 106 |
| Depreciation | 35 | 3 | 0 | 38 | 65 | 103 |
| Utilities | 28 | 0 | 0 | 28 | 65 | 93 |
| Insurance | 2 | 0 | 0 | 2 | 5 | 7 |
| Worship | 96 | 0 | 38 | 134 | 0 | 134 |
| Education | 12 | 0 | 0 | 12 | 0 | 12 |
| Professional Fees | 0 | 0 | 0 | 0 | 23 | 23 |
| Communications | 0 | 0 | 0 | 0 | 25 | 25 |
| Other | 0 | 0 | 0 | 0 | 159 | 159 |
| Total Expenses | $ 354 | $ 48 | $ 253 | $ 655 | $ 447 | $ 1,102 |

Finally, there is the Statement of Functional Expenses (Exhibits 3-4 and 3-5). Earlier in this chapter we learned that the Statement of Financial Position, Statement of Activities, and Statement of Cash Flows exist but have different titles in the audited financial statements of for-profit organizations. The Statement of Functional Expenses is unique to the nonprofit world. It provides details on where the organization spent money during each of the most recent fiscal years. Like the Statement of Activities and the Statement of Cash Flows, the Statement of Functional Expenses illustrates the movement of resources during a period of time. It shows by broad category where Any Church spent its money.

The Statement of Functional Expenses breaks down the expenses of Any Church in a matrix format, attributing types of expenses (compensation, housing, etc.) incurred to support programs and pay for overhead. The process of expense allocation can differ among organizations, so any conclusions from information in the Statement of Functional Expenses should be guarded. The Statement of Functional Expenses enjoys an interactive relationship with the Statement of Activities. The total expenses Any Church incurred in 2020 and 2019 of $1,102,000 and $1,089,000 listed in its Statement of Functional Expenses matches the expenses listed in the Statement of Financial Position (Exhibit 3-2).

## Summary

When clergy and lay members accept a position on the governing body of their congregation, they discover they have been dealt a challenging hand of financial cards. Church leaders have all of the responsibility for the financial conduct of their church but lack, due to a number of practical considerations, the authority to change some aspects of their church's financial practices. They have agency, but their freedom to exercise that agency is circumscribed by accounting conventions and the expectations of third parties. This is a disquieting, but unavoidable, aspect of church leadership.

Church leaders learn to focus their energy on financial matters where their agency is active and their influence can make a practical difference. This task is not made easier by differences in the vocabulary of for-profit and nonprofit finance. Because of these differences, it is sometimes the church leaders with a background in for-profit financial matters who have difficulty absorbing the nuances of this new vocabulary.

Church leaders don't have to become financial experts, but they do need a working knowledge of the church's audited financial statements. The four financial reports that comprise the audited financial statements are not static, standalone documents. They interact with one another in important ways. Understanding the nature of that interaction can lead to a better appreciation of the church's financial profile overall.

When it comes to financial reporting, church leaders can spend their time productively on the repurposing of existing information, the creation of new information, and the distribution of information to the stakeholders of their church. A church's stakeholder universe goes well beyond current membership, and includes donors, governments, regulators, partner organizations, employees, and denominational authorities, among others. Voluntarily distributing the church's financial and operating information is a novel and uncomfortable proposition for many church leaders.

## Questions to Consider

1. How important is having audited financial statements with a clean opinion to your church?

2. Do you understand the central purpose of each of the four financial reports in your church's audited financial statements?

3. How receptive is your membership to disclosing church financial information that could be accessed by nonmembers?

# 4 · Capital, Capitalization, Capital Formation, and Endowments

> Command them to do good, to be rich in good deeds, and to be generous and willing to share. In this way they will lay up treasure for themselves as a firm foundation for the coming age, so that they may take hold of the life that is truly life.
>
> —1 Timothy 6:18–19

## Capital in a Church

People don't often use the words "church" and "capital" in the same sentence except, perhaps, in a church capital campaign. Most folks don't think "church" and "capital" have much in common. In fact, "capital" is a word with multiple meanings. It adds another layer of opaqueness to conversations about church finance.

The availability of financial capital has a significant effect on the ability of a church to pursue its mission. As we will explore further in chapter 9, a church cannot sustain its operations, and therefore its mission, unless it generates capital on a consistent basis at a rate greater than inflation. Financial capital enables a congregation to hire staff, support existing programs, and start new programs. Church leaders need a fulsome understanding of the term "capital." They also must develop an appreciation of the deep connection between "capital" and "mission."

What does the term "capital" mean in a church context? Capital is the resources the church has at its disposal to provide services to its members and the world. Capital is not just cash and investments, although financial assets are critical components of church capital. Capital includes inventory, goodwill, buildings, and property. Capital also includes intangible assets, such as reputation in the local community, that are not captured by accounting methodologies. Capital can be thought of as all the tools a church has acquired at a point in time to pursue its mission.

We can refine the definition of church capital into a useful shorthand for purposes of conversations regarding church money matters. Capital is the sum of resources a church has acquired at a point in time *where the economic value of those resources is easily determined*. Once the notion of convenience is introduced into the mix, the information contained in a church's Statement of Financial Position serves as a useful shorthand for church capital. It's not technically correct, but it's close enough and is easy to understand.

Exhibit 4-1

**Any Church · Capitalization**

|  | Dec. 31, 2020 |
|---|---|
| Cash & Equivalents | $ 219,000 |
| Investments | $ 3,906,000 |
| Property & Equipment (Net) | $ 1,299,000 |
| **Total Capital** | **$ 5,424,000** |
| Debt | $ 3,000 |
| Restricted Gifts | $ 3,614,000 |
| Surplus & Unrestricted Gifts | $ 1,807,000 |
| **Total Capitalization** | **$ 5,424,000** |

Using this shorthand, church capital equals the total assets listed in the Statement of Financial Position. Let's return to the financial statements of Any Church. When we use this definition of capital, Exhibit 4-1 indicates that as of December 31, 2020, the capital of Any Church totaled $5,424,000, consisting of cash ($219,000), investments ($3,906,000), and property and equipment ($1,299,000).

This definition of capital is flawed because it does not consider the value of intangible assets. The bookkeeping system of a church is not designed to capture intangible assets, even though intangible assets have real economic value. The most obvious example is volunteer labor. Volunteer labor is critical in the day-to-day operations of most churches. Imagine the cost to your church if it had to pay market rates for the all the work performed by its members without charge. The problem is that *the economic value of voluntary labor is not easily determined.* It can be estimated, but not easily or with much precision.

Reputational capital is another important asset many churches possess. Reputation can be the determining factor in receiving a line of credit from a bank or a grant from a foundation. As is the case with volunteer labor, the economic value of reputational capital is not easily determined. Reputational capital can be estimated, but not easily or with much precision.

A church's Statement of Financial Position does not reflect these and other intangible assets because they are not captured by standard accounting methodologies. For this reason, using the assets in the Statement of Financial Position as a proxy for church capital may understate the resources a church can access to pursue its mission. Despite this deficiency, the assets listed in this financial statement are an acceptable surrogate for conversations about church capital.

### Capitalization of a Church

A church's capital structure explains how a church paid for its assets. If someone asks how a church is capitalized, they are asking how much of the church's capital structure comes from each source of funds. Every church has a capital structure, although church leadership may not realize it. As Clara Miller asserts, "Capital structure is sometimes invisible but never absent."[1] Capital structure—capitalization—is the mix of financing alternatives a church uses to accumulate its tangible assets.

The capital structure or capitalization of Any Church appears on the lower portion of its Statement of Financial Position (see Exhibit 4-1). Churches pay for their assets or capital through some combination of borrowing, gifts, and savings. Any Church paid for its $5,424,000 of church capital through modest borrowing ($3,000), restricted gifts ($3,614,000), and a combination of cumulative surpluses plus unre-

---

1   Clara Miller, "Hidden in Plain Sight: Understanding Capital Structure," NPQ, March 21, 2003, https://nonprofitquarterly.org/hidden-in-plain-sight-understanding-capital-structure/.

stricted gifts ($1,807,000). Because our shorthand definition of capital excludes assets where the value cannot be easily determined, church capital (assets) will always equal the sum of its borrowings, gifts, and cumulative savings.

## Assembling a Capital Structure in a Church

In the for-profit world, where the primary objective is to increase shareholder value, significant time and attention is devoted to reducing the cost of capital. This is particularly true in the realm of publicly held companies where a lower cost of capital can create a competitive advantage. The finance staff in these organizations tries to assemble a mix of financing sources that minimizes the overall cost of capital while managing the risk that borrowed capital (debt) comes with repayment obligations that may be difficult to manage in the future.

Except in the most prosperous congregations, managing the cost of capital is not a pressing concern for a church. This is not because churches wouldn't benefit if they could lower their cost of capital. It is because most churches have very few options when it comes to financing alternatives.[2] So spending time trying to lower capital costs, for many congregations, is not worth the lift. Most church capital structures are more a function of history and serendipity than active management.

Why do churches have such limited financing options? Primarily because, unlike for-profit enterprises, churches are not owned. A church cannot raise permanent capital quickly by selling ownership interests. This means churches cannot tap into the markets for equity and equity-linked securities. The only way most churches can access funds quickly—and change their capital structure quickly—is to borrow (or repay borrowed) funds.

Not every church is credit worthy and not every church can incur

---

2   There are nonprofit organizations, particularly those that have accumulated significant Total Net Assets (Fund Balances), that have greater choice in assembling capital structure. Thad Calabrese has explored capital structure theories in some detail. See Thad D. Calabrese, "Testing Competing Capital Structure Theories of Nonprofit Organizations," *Public Budgeting and Finance*, September 14, 2011, https://onlinelibrary.wiley.com/doi/abs/10.1111/j.1540-5850.2011.00989.x, and Thad D. Calabrese, "The Accumulation of Nonprofit Profits: A Dynamic Analysis." *Nonprofit and Voluntary Sector Quarterly* 41, no. 2 (2011), https://journals.sagepub.com/doi/abs/10.1177/0899764011404080.

debt. Churches that can borrow often find that the terms and amount of capital are limited due to lender concerns. What bank wants the public relations nightmare that comes with foreclosing on a loan to a church? Many banks address this challenge by either not lending to churches, or by lending to churches on more restrictive terms than they offer to for-profit organizations with a similar credit profile. And even a church that is credit worthy and can borrow on reasonable terms has to keep in mind that debt must eventually be repaid.

The inability to sell ownership interests and the limited ability to incur debt means that few churches can actively manage their cost of capital. More importantly, it also means that the capital structure of most churches changes very slowly over time. When it changes, it's rarely because the church discovers a new source of capital. It changes because the church operates at a net surplus or net deficit. The only way most churches can improve their capital structure is by generating annual operating surpluses for an extended period of time. *This unavoidable reliance on internally generated capital creates an invisible, but very real, glass ceiling on a church's ability to pursue its mission.*

### Capital Formation in a Church

The limited number of financing options available to a church means that its mission depends heavily on the church's ability to generate a surplus from operations. Said another way, a church must consistently produce a profit from operations to pursue its mission. The idea that a church *must* make a profit in order to fulfill its missional goals is an uncomfortable revelation. Somehow this seems too worldly, if not downright un-Christian. Church leaders must learn to manage any anxiety they have about operating profitably. Generating profits on a consistent basis is an unavoidable task for a church truly committed to realizing its mission.

Exhibit 4-2

| Any Church · Capital Formation | Dec. 31, 2019 | Dec. 31, 2020 |
|---|---|---|
| Revenue | | |
| Contributions | $ 806,000 | $ 777,000 |
| Bequests | 0 | $ 450,000 |
| Other | $ 122,000 | $ 77,000 |
| **Total Revenue** | **$ 928,000** | **$ 1,304,000** |
| Expenses | | |
| Program Services | $ 649,000 | $ 655,000 |
| Management & General | $ 440,000 | $ 447,000 |
| **Total Expenses** | **$ 1,089,000** | **$ 1,102,000** |
| Change in Net Assets from Operations | (161,000) | 202,000 |
| Non-Operating Items | | |
| Realized Gains (Losses) on Investments | $ 37,000 | $ 34,000 |
| Unrealized Gains (Losses) on Investments | $ 12,000 | (225,000) |
| Loss on Sale of Property & Equipment | 0 | (26,000) |
| **Change in Net Assets** | **$ (112,000)** | **$ (15,000)** |
| Net Assets | | |
| Beginning of Year | $ 5,548,000 | $ 5,436,000 |
| End of Year | $ 5,436,000 | $ 5,421,000 |

In 2020 the ability of Any Church to realize its mission was materially compromised by its results from operations. This development may not be immediately apparent in Exhibit 4-2, which shows a surplus from operations of $202,000. (This exhibit should look familiar; it contains the same information we encountered in Exhibit 3-2 in chapter 3.) A close reading reveals that this surplus was only made possible by a bequest of $450,000. Bequests are wonderful events that should be encouraged and celebrated. Operating at a deficit and balancing the books on the back of a bequest, however, is not evidence of sustainable financial practices. The church leaders of Any Church were saved by nonprofit accounting conventions. Recall from chapter 3 that all types of revenues, regardless of their source, are recognized in the Statement of Activities. Due to this accounting convention—not good financial management—the proceeds from the bequest are included in the calculation of income from operations, despite the fact that bequests have nothing to do with current operations.

If we exclude the bequest, Any Church actually experienced a loss from operations of $248,000 ($202,000 as reported adjusted for this $450,000 one-time event). After taking into account nonoperating items, Any Church should have realized a total loss of $465,000 in 2020. This would have resulted in a reduction of net assets between 2019 and 2020 of $465,000. This reduction in net assets would be reflected in the net assets without donor restrictions account, which would have declined by over 25 percent. Fortunately, Any Church is a wealthy congregation. If the bequest had never been received, Any Church would still have just under $5,000,000 in net assets at the end of 2020.

Managing the affairs of the church in 2021, however, would have become considerably more challenging. The mix of unrestricted to restricted assets would decline from 33/67 percent to 27/73 percent. This shift to a more restricted net asset base could compromise management's ability to meet the church's expenses, depending on the restrictions that govern the church's restricted assets. And, as Exhibit 4-2 also reveals, this loss from operations comes on the back of a $161,000 loss from operations the previous year. Were it not for the $450,000 bequest, the financial position of Any Church would have deteriorated meaningfully during the past two years.

### Endowments in a Church

The terms of the bequest that buffered Any Church's financial performance aren't disclosed in its financial statements. But the appearance of this gift itself introduces another component of capital structure found in many churches—endowments. Technically, the term "endowment" refers only to a true endowment, the earnings from which are restricted according to terms imposed by the donor. Exhibit 4-1 indicates that Any Church has $3,614,000 in restricted (true) endowment.

Church leaders typically think of endowment as all of the financial assets that have been set aside to support the operations of the church, regardless of restrictions.[3] Using this more popular definition, endowment also includes permanent funds where restrictions can be modified (technically, quasi-endowment) or where there are no restrictions (technically, funds functioning as endowment). In a church setting, when someone says endowment, they typically mean *all* of the funds whose corpus must be maintained, but whose earnings are available to pay the expenses of the church. According to this popular definition, Exhibit 4-1 indicates that Any Church has $5,421,000 ($3,614,000 plus $1,807,000) in endowment.

A church cannot use earnings from donor-restricted (true) endowment for purposes other than those designated by the donor. For example, a true endowment could be established to purchase flowers to decorate the church on Sundays. Earnings from this endowment could only be used to purchase flowers. If the deed of gift restricted earnings to enhance Sunday morning services, rather than just purchase flowers, the earnings could be used to purchase flowers but could also be used in other ways that might improve the Sunday worship experience. The restrictions that come with true endowments limit the financial flexibility church leaders possess in managing the financial affairs of the organization. Churches blessed with significant true endowments can be lulled into a false sense of comfort about their ability to meet financial obligations in the near term due to these restrictions.

Quasi-endowments are permanent funds restricted by the church governing body rather than the donor. The application of earnings from quasi-endowments are constrained just like earnings from donor-restricted endowments, and the restrictions must be honored. The difference is that the governing body of the church can change or eliminate the restrictions at its discretion. For example, a church could set aside financial assets in 2020 to grow its youth program. Earnings from these funds could only be used to pay the compensation costs of a youth minister and the other costs of the youth program. If church leaders decide in 2025 to deemphasize the youth program, the governing board in 2025 can lift the restrictions on these funds and spend the earnings elsewhere.

---

3 Endowments can take other forms, notably real estate. A parking garage, for example, could serve as endowment.

Unrestricted endowments are permanent funds where the earnings can be used by the church for any lawful purpose. Gifts of permanent funds where the donors did not impose restrictions on the use of the earnings are reflected here. Net assets without donor restrictions is also where operating surpluses generated by the church accumulate. This is also where equity in fixed assets and other nonliquid forms of permanent capital appear. The $1,807,000 of net assets without donor restrictions on Any Church's statement of financial position is likely a combination of different assets, only a portion of which function as an endowment in the popular sense of the word.

Every endowment is a welcome addition to the capital structure of a church. True endowments are a blessing, but by definition, are less flexible than quasi- or unrestricted endowments. Difficulties arise when the gift instrument associated with a restricted endowment limits the use of earnings to an activity the church no longer requires. This can occur whenever a church reimagines its mission. It almost always occurs in older congregations, which benefit from endowments that were established in the distant past. Apocryphal stories from these communities, like the true endowment established to encourage clergy to make pastoral visits through the purchase of buggy whips, are not uncommon.

Endowments have a dark side when they create a false sense of financial security in a church. As we've discovered, Any Church is blessed with total endowment of $5,421,000. This is a significant amount of permanent capital for what appears to be a medium size congregation, judging by the amount of contributions it receives from its members ($777,000 in 2020 according to Exhibit 4-2).

We've also observed that the mix between restricted and unrestricted assets at Any Church is shifting toward restricted assets. If not for a sizeable bequest, Any Church would have seen the percentage of its total net assets with donor restrictions grow meaningfully in 2020. In spite of a healthy amount of total permanent capital, the ability of Any Church to meet its immediate needs will be compromised if this trend continues. We know from the Statement of Functional Expenses that compensation accounts for almost 40 percent of Any Church's total expenses (see Exhibit 3-5). If you add housing and benefits, the personnel costs of Any Church account for over half of all the church's expenses.

If the terms of Any Church's donor-restricted assets don't permit earnings to pay compensation costs, Any Church may soon be pressed to meet its obligations to clergy and staff. Put another way, Any Church might remain "statement of financial position rich" but could become "statement of activities poor" in the near future if it is restricted from spending the earnings from the largest portion of its endowment where it needs them most. The church leaders at Any Church might find themselves legally restricted from paying compensation expenses despite having the cash to meet these obligations.

## Summary

Church capital consists of all of the assets a church collects to realize its mission. Unfortunately, accounting systems are not designed to capture and value some important church assets, such as volunteer labor. When it comes to discussing church capital, church leaders may find it expedient to define church capital simply as the assets listed on the Statement of Financial Position.

Churches have very few ways to attract the capital they need to realize their mission. Like other nonprofits, churches cannot sell an equity interest in the organization. A church can only borrow capital, receive capital as a gift, or save capital from earnings. Borrowing can help address cash needs in the short run, but borrowing is not a long-term solution because debt must be repaid. Large gifts are wonderful but are episodic and difficult to predict. The only method a church has under its control to increase its capital base or change its capitalization is to operate profitably annually and save a portion of its surplus every year.

Endowments help stabilize a church's capital base. Endowed churches enjoy a more diversified revenue stream that makes budgeting and financial planning easier. Church leaders must make sure, however, that they understand any restrictions on these endowments. Donor restrictions may prohibit the church from meeting all of its current obligations. The amount of total net assets a church has at its disposal can induce a false sense of security.

## Questions to Consider

1. How is your church capitalized?

2. If the growth in unrestricted net assets your church has experienced over the past five years continues, will your church be able to realize its mission over the next five years?

3. If your church has true endowments, have annual earnings ever not been spent because of restrictions associated with those endowments?

# 5 · Budgets and Budgeting

> "Suppose one of you wants to build a tower. Won't you first sit down and estimate the cost to see if you have enough money to complete it? For if you lay the foundation and are not able to finish it, everyone who sees it will ridicule you, saying, 'This person began to build and wasn't able to finish.'"
>
> —Luke 14:28–30

## Budgets

The church financial statements described in the previous three chapters are all backwards-looking documents. They are the offspring of convention and accounting methodologies, describing the financial state of a church as it was in the past. Budgets are a different kind of creature. A budget is a forward-looking document—a set of financial projections designed to compare the actual financial performance of a church in future periods against anticipated results.

There are different kinds of budgets. The two budgets commonly used in a church are capital budgets and operating budgets. Capital budgets are used to monitor planned investments in large, expensive assets such as equipment and buildings. Operating budgets forecast revenues and expenses associated with running the church. When people refer to *the* budget in a church context, they are referring to the operating budget. This chapter is concerned with the creation and application of operating budgets.

## Why Budgets Matter

Budgets are part of twenty-first century church life. According to the National Study of Congregations' Economic Practices, 91 percent of churches have formal written budgets.[1] Regardless of a church's size, budgets are considered *prima facie* evidence of good organizational hygiene. One reason churches have a budget is because of a widely held notion that an organization without a budget isn't a serious organization. Like many other aspects of a church's financial life, budgets derive much of their authority from social convention. Popular wisdom is that churches should budget, and so they do.

This expectation may stem from the usefulness of a well-crafted budget as a control document. A good budget enables church leaders to monitor the financial status of the church on a semi-regular basis. Budgets serve as an important management tool for any kind of organization because they can be used to hold people and programs more accountable on the basis of interim financial results. Budgets help facilitate conversations about midcourse corrections in nonemotional terms.

A good budget is particularly valuable in monitoring and proactively managing a church's cash position. A church that lacks sufficient cash cannot function effectively. A church that lacks sufficient cash for an extended period won't be around to meet its missional objectives. Monthly budgets provide insight into current and upcoming events that might affect a church's cash position. This insight can help church leaders to respond proactively to the church's immediate cash needs.

Church budgets retain their utility in future periods. A church's track record on meeting or falling short of its budgetary goals matters to church stakeholders and potential stakeholders. Church members want to know that the organization is generally healthy, and the ability to meet budget objectives over time provides evidence of good financial management. Donors—particularly large donors—want assurance that the church will be a good steward of their gifts. Meeting or exceeding budget goals on a consistent basis is also evidence of good stewardship. There are a host of external parties, including banks, foundations, and independent evaluators, whose willingness to assist a church pursue its mission will be influenced by the organization's historical record of achieving its financial projections.

---

1   Mark Chaves and Alison Eagle, *Religious Congregations in 21st Century America: National Congregations Study 2015* (Chicago: Giving USA Foundation, 2015), 33.

Budgets serve as an important management tool and communications medium for any nonprofit organization. Budgets also provide a unique function in a church setting. A new budget represents the next step toward meeting God's mission envisioned by *this* church. Nimi Wariboko, a former professor at Andover Newton Seminary, famously declared that "budget is theology." Wariboko explained, "The budget of a church points to its deepest commitments. The budget as an indicator of the economic power of the church expresses its concept of what it means to do the work of Christ, to witness the gospel or execute the greatest and holiest work of the Church. The budget expresses the mission of the church."[2]

Budgets matter in churches because they articulate the immediate, next steps the church plans to take in pursuit of its ultimate goals. Budgets demythologize lofty ambitions by defining in concrete terms what the clergy and lay leaders of a church believe are the actions the church must take in the near term to realize its ambitions. Budgets are an embodied wake-up call that is difficult to ignore: if church leaders can't demonstrate that the current budget, if met, will advance the church's mission, either the budget or the mission needs to be reconsidered.

### Budgeting

A budget is a document that is the culmination of a process known as budgeting. The process of budgeting is more consequential than the budget document it produces. There are three approaches to budgeting in a church. The least common approach is activity-based budgeting. Activity-based budgeting groups revenue and expense items according to the missional goals of the church, sorted by program. Inputs and outputs are program centric. The process of producing an activity-based budget can be very useful as part of a broader strategic planning exercise because activity-based budgets shine a light on the cost of each program. For this reason, activity-based budgets can provide important material for the creation of the supplemental financial information discussed in chapter 3.

---

2 Nimi Wariboko, *Accounting & Money for Ministerial Leadership* (Eugene, OR: Wipf & Stock, 2013), 66.

For purposes of monitoring a church's financial operations on a real-time basis, activity-based budgeting has limited value. Other kinds of nonprofit organizations, such as museums, have diversified revenue streams. The relative contribution of revenue from each line of business—each activity—is important to understand. Using the museum example, the revenue and expense associated with membership, special exhibits, food service, and concessions are easy to pair, so the contribution of each line of business to the organization's overall results can be analyzed and actions taken. Changes in the mix of activities are also important to understand.

Most churches receive the majority of their revenue from unrestricted donations. Although some contributions are reserved for certain applications, most church revenue is not program specific. In terms of product line and profitability analysis, church revenue and program expense are tethered to one another in very loose fashion. Any attempt to evaluate individual program effectiveness through activity-based budgeting is somewhat academic.

Another major complication that limits the appeal of activity-based budgeting for churches is the challenge of allocating indirect costs. Indirect costs, sometimes described as overhead, are the fixed costs of operating the church that do not vary with activity. (Efforts to allocate indirect costs can arise in any budget exercise, but they are unavoidable in activity-based budgeting.) Some indirect costs, such as real estate, are immoveable. Once incurred, they become financial obligations the church must satisfy independent of programmatic activity. Other indirect costs, such as janitorial services, are more variable. These costs are fixed in the sense that they cannot be eliminated, but the magnitude of these expenses may vary based on a variety of other factors.

Allocating costs is difficult and time consuming. There are no generally accepted guidelines to follow, so there are no objective criteria on what is fair. Inevitably, some group or program in the congregation will feel unduly burdened and want to protest their allocation. If the cost allocation process is perceived as arbitrary or inequitable, even by a vocal minority of the congregation, the legitimacy of the entire budget process may be called into question.

Activity-based budgeting works best where there is strong consensus about a church's mission and strong consensus about the best way to realize that mission. Consensus about mission, at a high level, may not be difficult to achieve. Getting the majority of a congregation to agree on the best way to achieve mission can be much more challenging. For all of these reasons, not many churches construct their operating budgets through activity-based budgeting.[3]

A more common approach, although still one not widely employed by churches, is known as zero-based budgeting. Zero-based budgeting ignores history. Instead, zero-based budgets are built each year from the ground up by allocating resources according to the values and goals of the church. Past experience is set aside. No arbitrary limits are placed on the amount of money that might be spent in particular categories.

For example, if one of the church's missional goals is to ensure food security for everyone who lives within ten blocks of the church, a zero-based budget will start by estimating whatever expenditures are necessary to feed the targeted population. Whatever was spent on food security last year is irrelevant; the only thing that matters is the current estimate of the cost to ensure the neighborhood's food security this year. The availability of church resources to meet this goal are taken into account as the budget evolves. Initially, however, projected program costs drive the budgeting process.

Zero-based budgeting works best in newly established churches. New churches are unburdened by tradition or precedent. For more established churches, zero-based budgeting is challenging. The good news is that zero-based budgeting forces church leaders to start each fiscal year with a fresh outlook. Their thinking, at least in theory, is not encumbered by what happened in the past. Zero-based budgeting is an intellectually honest way to approach financial planning. Sacred cows are stripped of their protected status and can be terminated with less emotional fallout.

---

3  John Wimberly makes a thoughtful case that churches should embrace activity-based costing, the centerpiece of activity-based budgeting, in his *The Business of the Church: The Uncomfortable Truth That Faithful Ministry Requires Effective Management* (Herndon, VA: Alban Institute, 2010).

Churches sometimes describe their budget to the congregation in terms of a "missional budget," illustrating what programs will receive financial support in the year ahead. This in most instances is a matter of presentation. The underlying process is not activity based, but instead reformats results from more conventional budget processes described below.

On the other hand, zero-based budgeting can hamper good financial planning because, by definition, it calls on church leaders to ignore the lessons of the recent past. It's difficult to accept the idea that what a church spent on a particular item or program last year has no bearing on what the church should consider spending on that same item or program next year. Whatever the church spent last year does influence what the individuals involved in budgeting think should be spent next year. Zero-based budgeting and this aspect of human nature coexist in a state of perpetual conflict.

Ignoring the lessons of recent history, which zero-based budgeting demands, will in the minds of some participants call into question the integrity of the budgeting exercise. Much like the process of cost allocation, anyone unhappy with the result will criticize the process as impractical or too theoretical. As a result, not many churches embrace zero-based budgeting. And even congregations that do find the approach appealing find it difficult to maintain over multiple annual budget cycles.

The vast majority of churches use what is called incremental budgeting to assemble an annual operating budget. Incremental budgeting examines each revenue and expense account in the church ledger, estimates what will be received or spent in each account during the current year, and projects what will be received or spent in each account incrementally next year. The process pivots off of recent actual experience. Accounts are classified according to type of transaction and are typically assigned a numeric code in something called a chart of accounts. Ideally, the work of incremental budgeting takes place at this granular, account-by-account level, although combining small accounts into summary categories is a practical interim step that won't by itself compromise the integrity of the budgeting process.

The budget is eventually rolled up into a document that mirrors a detailed version of the Statement of Activities. The document is subdivided by month so that actual performance can be compared to projected performance throughout the year. Rather than simply divide the total annual budget by twelve, seasonal adjustments to revenue and expense items can be factored in. For example, revenue from plate donations might be projected to rise in December and April around

Christmas and Easter, and fall during the summer months. As the year progresses, activity levels are adjusted to respond to any shortfall in revenue or expense overage.

## Why Budgeting Matters More than Budgets

How an organization goes about budgeting has practical ramifications that transcend the value of the budget document itself. The first is the role the process of budgeting can play in ensuring organizational alignment. The more a congregation's members—and its staff—are involved in the budgeting process, the greater the likelihood that the membership and staff will feel a sense of ownership in the resulting financial plan. Similarly, the earlier the budgeting process begins, the greater the opportunity for additional input, and the greater the likelihood that the organization as a whole will feel a sense of ownership in the budget.

There is a natural tension that mitigates against involving too many individuals and taking too much time to construct a budget. Some budgetary matters, particularly personnel matters, require a level of confidentiality that can't be maintained if the budget process casts too wide a net. Starting the budget process too early means that fewer months of current year results will be available to guide next year's budget conversations. And, of course, as important as a good budget may be, time spent on budgeting is time away from addressing today's challenges. Like so many financial activities, what constitutes good budgeting for a church will always be institution specific, but the value of involving more individuals and providing ample opportunity for them to provide input as a means of promoting widespread acceptance of the final budget should not be underestimated.

Widespread acceptance of the budget is critical in maintaining a church's financial discipline. The will of the organization to adhere to the budget will always be tested as the church conducts its operations and encounters financial challenges. Clergy, lay professional staff, and volunteers are less likely to take a parochial view on responses that negatively impact their areas of responsibility if they believe their views were taken into account when the budget was created and the congregation's priorities for the year financially represented. This can be especially important in times of financial crisis.

Perhaps the greatest value the process of budgeting provides is an annual reminder that church leaders must remain vigilant about achieving missional objectives. Budgeting, whatever form it takes, is the church's process for effecting a near-term plan that makes it possible to achieve the church's long-term goals. As Gil Rendle, senior advisor to the Texas Methodist Foundation, dryly observed, "It is one thing to know our mission. It is quite a different matter to discern what is required first and then subsequent steps must be put in place to move us closer to that central purpose."[4]

Church leaders make a mistake if they think of budgeting as a necessary evil, a tedious responsibility most effectively handled simply by marking up last year's budget in light of recent results. Budgeting is an opportunity to step back and consider whether the church is making progress—genuine progress—toward achieving its mission. If there is not consensus among church leaders that the proposed budget advances the mission, either the budget or the mission needs to be revisited.

### Budget, Mission, and Stewardship

There is an organic relationship between budget, mission, and stewardship. The budget is a congregation's near-term plan for realizing its long-term mission. Church members are stewards of God's resources. The church's budget provides each church member with a roadmap for returning to God a portion of his resources in their care. Why, then, do conversations about the relationship between budget, mission, and stewardship make church leaders so anxious?

Many stories in the Hebrew Bible and the New Testament concern the relationship between people and their possessions. The central theme that animates every "possessions" narrative can be summarized quite simply: God owns everything, and humans serve as trustees on God's behalf. Humans are God's stewards. They receive assets from God in the form of time, talent, and treasure. Each individual has complete discretion over how and where to invest God's assets, but must exercise the same care as if God's assets were their own. In other words, the

---

4   Gil Rendle, *Doing the Math of Mission: Fruits, Faithfulness, and Metrics* (Lanham, MD: Rowman & Littlefield, 2014), 57.

commission is not just to preserve God's assets, but to grow them. As Roman Catholic lay leader Kerry Robinson says:

> One definition of stewardship is the proper care for all that has been entrusted to one. That is hard enough to achieve, but for a person of faith, stewardship requires more. For a person of faith, stewardship is both the proper care of all that has been entrusted to one *and* the recognition of and response to the potential at hand.[5]

Church provides one outlet for an individual to realize this potential. A church with a compelling mission responds to the needs of God's world. So investing in that church and helping it achieve its mission is good stewardship. And because a budget describes in financial terms how the church plans to realize its mission, the connection between budget, mission, and stewardship becomes apparent.

Problems arise when the annual appeal or every member visitation kicks into high gear, and solicitors try to raise money to meet budget goals rather than to realize the mission. There is, of course, nothing inherently wrong with giving money to help meet the budget. But when the focus of solicitation conversations becomes budget-centric rather than mission-centric, the connection between the individual, charged only to be a good steward, and his or her church can begin to fray. After all, it's quite possible to be an extremely generous steward without giving one dollar to a particular church. Each church is but one of many vehicles where an individual can invest God's assets prudently.

Church leaders must make sure that budgets, and fundraising efforts to meet budgets, don't become an end in themselves. Budgets and budgeting are important tools for creating a sustainable church. They are, however, just tools. A church that conflates stewardship and mission with stewardship and budgets edges onto thin ice.

---

5   Kerry Alys Robinson, *Imagining Abundance* (Collegeville, MN: Liturgical Press, 2014), 34.

## Summary

Budgets come in many varieties. The kinds of budgets that churches use most frequently are capital budgets and operating budgets. Unless a church has significant property, plant, and equipment, or is undertaking a major renovation or building project, it may not need to create a capital budget. Almost all churches, however, produce an annual operating budget.

Operating budgets for churches come in different flavors. Activity-based budgets and zero-based budgets each have unique strengths, but neither has enjoyed much uptake in church settings. The vast majority of churches create their operating budgets incrementally, projecting revenue and expenses in light of recent experience.

Budgets are important. They create financial benchmarks that allow church leaders to monitor the financial condition of the church throughout the year. Analyzing the differences between actual versus budgeted performance after the fact can help church leaders budget more accurately in future periods. But the process of how a church budgets matters as much as the document the process produces. Enforcing a budget often involves restricting investments in projects or programs important to members and staff. Sometimes programs and projects must be eliminated altogether. Program champions may not like the consequences a budget has on their favorite activity, but they are much more likely to accept the consequences if they believe their voice has been heard in the budgeting process.

Inviting too many people into the budgeting process is inefficient. Budgeting too far in advance is ineffective because the results from the current year are preliminary. But the fact remains that the more people and time involved in budgeting, the more likely the organization will embrace the disciplines demanded by the budget. Budgeting is inevitably a balancing act, weighing investments of personnel and time against the need for congregational and staff support.

**Questions to Consider**

1. Based on the most recent five years, how have your church's actual results compared to your budget?

2. Is the annual budgeting process in your church "top down" or "bottom up" and who is involved?

3. Is your church a good steward of God's assets? How do you know?

# 6 · The Philanthropic Landscape

What I tell you in the dark, speak in the daylight; what
is whispered in your ear, proclaim from the roofs.

—Matthew 10:27

## Church Cheese

Churches compete with many deserving nonprofit organizations for
donations. Fortunately, Americans have both the capacity and willingness to be generous. According to the Giving USA Foundation,
Americans gave $450 billion to charity in 2019.[1] The potential finan-
cial support for charitable causes is plentiful, but even the wealthiest
individuals and foundations have resource constraints. Directly and
indirectly, churches compete with other nonprofit organizations for
these charitable dollars. The environment in which this competition
unfolds is called the philanthropic ecosystem.

For most of the twentieth century, the rules of engagement in the philanthropic ecosystem did not change. Participating organizations were
highly respectful of one another, generally reluctant to acknowledge
that a competition for dollars was taking place. Arguments for support
were grounded in the organization's unique identity. Appeals were often
based on the donor's loyalty to the institution and a sense of obligation.
Donors large and small assumed the organization could be trusted to
administer and spend their gifts wisely. These general rules of engagement—emphasizing uniqueness, loyalty, and obligation—worked well
for most mainstream religious organizations.

The philanthropic ecosystem has changed meaningfully over the
past two decades. The competitive nature of the chase for charitable

---

1 Giving USA Foundation, *Giving USA 2020: The Annual Report on Philanthropy for
the Year 2019* (Chicago: Giving USA Foundation, 2020), 22.

dollars has come out from the shadows and into the open. Arguments for support are now frequently based on relative performance and specific goals. Donor behavior has become more complex, based less on a sense of obligation and more on a desire to make a difference. Donors expect more frequent interaction with their charities. The willingness of large donors to make substantial commitments without the ability to revise their level of support is on the wane.

In this zero-sum game landscape, winners and losers have begun to emerge. Education, for example, is among the winners. According to the Giving USA Foundation, aggregate gifts to education increased $21.8 billion or 59 percent between 1998 and 2018. The subcategory of higher education is doing particularly well. In 2018, forty-eight colleges and universities were conducting billion-dollar-plus capital campaigns. That same year, ten other colleges and universities successfully completed billion-dollar-plus capital campaigns.[2]

Religious organizations have not fared so well during this period. Giving to religion remains the largest recipient category for charitable dollars, as it has since the Giving USA Foundation began publishing its surveys in the 1950s. In 2018, gifts to religion totaled $125 billion, or 29 percent of all charitable giving. However, the growth in gifts to religious causes only increased $19.4 billion or 18 percent between 1998 and 2018. The result is a meaningful loss in the relative market share of charitable gift by religion from just twenty years ago, when religious institutions accounted for 37 percent of all charitable contributions.

Some congregations have bucked this trend and still enjoy significant financial support from their members. As a category, however, religious giving is losing the contest for donor's wallets. Houses of worship are receiving a smaller and smaller share of each charitable dollar. When it comes to charitable giving, to borrow Spencer Johnson's famous trope, the church's cheese has moved.

---

2   Giving USA Foundation, *Giving USA 2019: The Annual Report on Philanthropy for the Year 2018* (Chicago: Giving USA Foundation, 2019), 203–4.

## Why Did the Cheese Move?

Changes in the philanthropic ecosystem—and the inability or unwillingness of churches to respond to these changes—partially account for religion's loss in wallet share. Two unrelated developments profoundly affected the world of nonprofit fundraising over the past two decades: the giving habits of a number of ultra-wealthy technology entrepreneurs, and the federal government's response to a series of accounting and financial scandals at a number of public companies. In combination, these events changed the way the wealthiest donors interacted with some highly visible charities. Over time, the relationship between less wealthy donors and less visible charitable institutions began to evolve along similar lines. Eventually, these new rules of engagement spread throughout the philanthropic ecosystem.

During this same period, the rise of secularism accelerated. As described in chapter 1, many churches were experiencing a decline in membership. Fewer members translated into fewer giving units, creating downward pressure on church revenue. The financial headwinds that come from fewer giving units were obvious to church leadership. Less obvious was the influence these cultural and regulatory events would eventually have on church donor behavior. Because churches tap into the pool of potential donors shared by all charitable institutions, the dynamic of church giving was destined to feel the effect of these macro developments.

Many other technology entrepreneurs amassed large personal fortunes during the 1980s and 1990s. West Coast financiers such as George Roberts, Pam and Pierre Omidyar, Melinda and Bill Gates, and other successful owner/operators then decided to turn their attention toward charitable activities at a relatively young age. They embarked on second careers as philanthropists.

In large measure, the companies they lead as operating executives were financed by West Coast–based venture capital firms. The venture capital business model at the time generally called for investing a small amount of money in a large number of companies. The overall failure rate of these venture-backed start-ups was high, but those that succeeded had the potential to generate massive investment gains for their financial sponsors. These venture investors managed the risk of failure by investing in multiple companies and limiting the amount of money they initially invested in each company.

Monitoring investments in a large portfolio of start-up companies based on different technologies necessitated the development of a common analytical framework. The progress made by these small companies had to be measured in both absolute terms and relative terms. Venture capital firms embraced the rigorous application of operating and financial metrics, applied across the portfolio, as the centerpiece of their approach to monitor their portfolio and to evaluate new investment opportunities. When investing in a new business, the initial investment decision might be made on the jockey (the entrepreneur) or the horse (promising technology).

Companies that made progress toward their goals would invariably need more money to fuel their growth. The evaluation process for additional investment was similar to the monitoring process: objective, quantitative, and heavily reliant on financial and operating metrics. Progress against a company's original business plan was taken into account, as well as its projected plan going forward. The venture firms could either increase their financial exposure by providing more funds or eliminate additional financial exposure by declining the opportunity to invest further. Companies that demonstrated potential would receive funding to support operations for another period, when the cycle would begin again.

This "wash-rinse-repeat" style of investing had a profound impact on the first generation of high-tech executives turned philanthropists. The investment vehicles they created to meet society's needs, such as The Omidyar Network and The Gates Foundation, embraced a highly analytical, metrics-centric approach to their work. (This trend continues with the establishment in 2015 of The Chan Zuckerberg Initiative by Facebook founder Mark Zuckerberg and his wife, Dr. Priscilla Chan, and the commitment in 2018 by Amazon founder Jeff Bezos to the Bezos Day One Fund.) Regardless of their specific areas of charitable interest, the manner in which this new generation of philanthropists began to practice philanthropy reflected the analytical framework they had experienced during their careers as high-tech operating executives.[3]

This new approach to philanthropic engagement has earned various labels, including catalytic philanthropy, impact investing, and venture philanthropy. This style of charitable investment began to spread throughout the philanthropic ecosystem in the first few years of the New Millennium. Katherine Fulton and Andrew Blau described it this way in 2005: "This so-called high-engagement philanthropy, born of efforts to incorporate successful practices from the venture capital industry into philanthropy, brings the donor and grantee into partnership in which the donor's money is allied with other assistance, and where the achievement of measurable goals is carefully tracked."[4]

These developments are interesting to historians of philanthropy, but how are they relevant to church leaders in the third decade of the new millennium? They are relevant because this new way of engaging with donors has found its way into all corners of the nonprofit ecosystem over the past twenty years. The particulars of how and why this change took place would take us down sideroads that aren't worth visiting. The thing church leaders must internalize is that, independent of giving capacity, donor expectations regarding how the nonprofit organizations they support should engage with them has fundamentally changed. The change began in one region with a handful of ultra-wealthy philanthropists. But the emphasis these individuals placed on metrics and performance now permeates the philanthropic ecosystem in which churches operate. This shift in emphasis affects all donors, including church donors.

A series of accounting and financial reporting scandals involving large public companies took place in the early 2000s that may have added momentum to this trend. WorldCom, Enron, Adelphia Communications, and others engaged in fraudulent practices that lead to

---

3   I am not suggesting technology entrepreneurs invented the metrical approach toward philanthropy; rather they helped popularize it, particularly on the West Coast. A similar reliance on metrics as a prerequisite for philanthropic engagement developed a few years later on the East Coast, led by individuals who accumulated significant wealth in finance services.

4   Katherine Fulton and Andrew Blau, *Looking Out for the Future: An Orientation for Twenty-First Century Philanthropists* (Cambridge, MA: Monitor Company Group, LLP, 2005), 24, https://community-wealth.org/sites/clone.community-wealth.org/files/downloads/report-fulton-blau.pdf.

massive financial losses. A series of congressional hearings followed, eventually resulting in new legislation designed to protect investors by improving financial disclosure and preventing accounting fraud. Transparency around goals and performance became the watchword among nonprofit and for-profit organizations alike.

The most consequential of these was The American Competitiveness and Corporate Accountability Act, also known as Sarbanes-Oxley or Sar-Box, which was enacted in 2002. Sarbanes-Oxley consists of seven main provisions designed to promote better corporate conduct and governance practices. Although the fraudulent activities that lead to the passage of Sarbanes-Oxley took place exclusively among large, for-profit companies, nonprofit organizations were swept up into Washington's legislative response.

Only two of the seven main provisions of Sarbanes-Oxley were intended to apply to the nonprofit world: the protection of whistleblowers and the prohibition against document destruction. Nonprofit organizations were not referenced in the other five provisions. Yet over time, virtually all of the Sarbanes-Oxley provisions found their way into the practices of charitable organizations that reside in the philanthropic ecosystem.

Precisely how this took place is not well understood. It may have occurred because board members of large for-profit organizations also served as board members of large nonprofit organizations. Compliance with Sarbanes-Oxley provisions became top-of-mind through their for-profit board service. Perhaps they concluded that the Sarbanes-Oxley provisions that specifically applied only to for-profit organizations would be good financial behavior for any organization, regardless of tax status. (Take, for example, Section 302 of Sarbanes-Oxley, which requires that senior management of a for-profit organization certify the accuracy of the organization's financial statements. Why shouldn't the senior management of the symphony, or university, or museum be willing to certify the financial statements of their organization be accurate?) For whatever reasons, many larger, prestigious nonprofit organizations began adopting more of the Sarbanes-Oxley provisions into their financial practices. Over time, less prestigious nonprofits with fewer high-profile board members began to follow suit.

In 2006, the Uniform Law Commission published recommended language for adoption by state governments regarding investment decisions and spending policies for endowed nonprofit institutions. The Uniform Prudent Management of Institutional Funds Act, known as UPMIFA legislation, which required heightened disclosure regarding the status of all endowed funds held by any nonprofit organization, was eventually passed in all fifty states and the District of Columbia. The result was renewed focus at even the smallest organizations on record-keeping and disclosure around gifts and spending policies.

The emergence of a generation of ultrawealthy, metrics-oriented philanthropists, combined with a series of federal and state laws demanding greater transparency and disclosure, shook the philanthropic ecosystem. Quantitative analysis, metrics, and relative performance became best practice for managing and monitoring the results of nonprofit organizations. Large, visible nonprofit organizations had no choice but to adopt a more open and quantitative worldview. The type of information this approach produced soon found its way into communications with important stakeholders, particularly donors and potential donors. Over the first two decades of the new millennium, nonprofits of all sizes eventually began to feel the tremors of these tectonic changes in the nonprofit landscape and began to respond.

Donor expectations regarding the amount and kinds of information they were entitled to receive from charities began to change. The availability of financial and operating Form 990 information from the IRS in a readable digital format, as described in chapter 3, couldn't have come at a more propitious time. Over time, this change in expectations began to affect the nature of the donor/charity relationship. As nonprofits provided more information on their performance more frequently in more transparent ways, donor standards regarding communication and engagement changed. By the beginning of the third decade of the new millennium, the cheese moved at many nonprofit organizations.

## Where Is the Church Cheese?

To date, the vast majority of churches in the United States have sidestepped this transparency revolution. One reason is that most churches are small, nonprofit organizations. The changes in the philanthropic ecosystem originated with large, secular foundation or foundation-style philanthropies. These changes were amplified by federal legislation aimed at large public companies. According to the National Study of Congregations' Economic Practices (NSCEP), a survey conducted by the Lake Institute of Faith and Giving, the median size congregation generates $169,000 in revenue.[5] As nonsecular, small, nonprofit organizations, most churches were unaffected in the early years.

The NSCEP estimates that 34 percent of all churches have endowments. By 2010, the passage of the UPMIFA laws began to drag churches into the movement toward greater disclosure and transparency.[6] Churches with restricted endowments had to provide their independent auditors with more information regarding these funds in order to receive a clean opinion on their audited financial statements. In some instances, churches responded by reviewing and improving their disclosure practices beyond just the realm of restricted endowment funds mandated by UPMIFA.

Many churches, however, did only what was required by UPMIFA. They elected not to use UPMIFA as a springboard into the growing movement toward a greater emphasis on quantitative analysis and metrics. Why? Perhaps some church leaders were unaware that the broader landscape of charitable fundraising was changing. Some may have been aware the environment was changing, but believed people gave to their church for entirely different reasons and therefore making additional changes was unnecessary. They may have reasoned that parroting the actions of other kinds of nonprofit organizations—becoming more analytical and transparent—would provide answers to questions that weren't being asked in church, a waste of time and resources.

It seems likely that many churches chose not to build upon UPMIFA's convenient call to action because of their reluctance to discuss the relationship between money and mission. As described in chapter 1, the resistance to discuss money matters in church is pervasive. Linking money to mission by benchmarking a church's financial performance

---

5   David P. King, Christopher W. Munn, Brad R. Fulton, and Jamie L. Goodwin, "The National Study of Congregations' Economic Practices," NSCEP, September 16, 2019, 14, https://www.nscep.org/wp-content/uploads/2019/09/Lake_NSCEP_09162019-F-LR.pdf.

6   Ibid., 16.

on a consistent basis—and reporting on outcomes versus plan in a highly transparent fashion—can't happen in a church unwilling to acknowledge the role money plays in realizing mission. Consequently, most endowed churches simply complied with UPMIFA's minimum standards. Will a minimalist disclosure strategy serve a church well over the next decade? The rising trend of income inequality in the United States suggests that all nonprofit organizations will become more reliant on a shrinking pool of potential donors. If this trend continues, fewer Americans are likely to control more of the national wealth. Fewer Americans will likely account for more of the dollars given to any charity. As other nonprofit organizations respond to this trend, trying to differentiate themselves from their competitors, this critical pool of wealthy donors will become accustomed to receiving information on absolute and relative performance. If members really do give to their church for different reasons than they give to other nonprofit institutions, then church leaders may not need to respond to developments in the donor marketplace. In light of the shift away from giving to religion in the new millennium identified by Giving USA, a decision not to respond could have serious consequences.

### Who Accounts for Most of the Church Cheese?

The giving preferences of individuals are of vital interest to churches because the average church receives 81 percent of its revenue from household contributions.[7] Although churches receive income from a variety of other sources, the financial viability of almost all churches depends on the generosity of its individual members—and a shrinking number of households are determining which tax-exempt organizations will receive funding.

In 2015, the IRS published a study of the change in charitable deductions on tax returns filed from 2003 to 2013 by income level. For this ten-year period, every income bracket below $100,000 reported a decline in charitable giving, ranging from 17 to 57 percent. Every income bracket above $100,000 reported an increase in charitable giving, ranging from

---

7  Ibid., 12.

20 to 104 percent. Charitable deductions for households with incomes of $100,000 or more increased approximately 40 percent during this ten-year period.[8] As charitable donations from households in lower income brackets shrink, and charitable donations from households in higher income brackets rise, the relative dependence of nonprofits on households in higher income brackets becomes more acute.

Changes in income tax policy has added momentum to these developments. The Tax Cuts and Jobs Act of 2017 (TCJA), among other things, reduced the incentives for millions of Americans to itemize charitable deductions on their tax returns. The TCJA increased the standard deduction for single individuals and couples filing separately from $6,350 to $12,000 and for couples filing jointly from $12,700 to $24,000. Starting in 2018, only Americans who donated amounts in excess of the standard deduction continued to enjoy the tax benefits available through itemizing.

In 2017, roughly one-third of all U.S. households filed itemized tax returns. Congress estimated that the TJCA would reduce this to just 12 percent of households.[9] The long-term implications of the TCJA are unknown, but the loss of economic incentive for millions of Americans to donate could be consequential for organizations that rely on small donations. If fewer lower- and middle-income households donate to charity, an even greater percentage of charitable contributions will inevitably come from the wealthiest households.

There is evidence the increasing dominance of wealthy households in charitable giving had accelerated by the time the coronavirus pandemic arrived in 2020. In an April 2020 poll conducted by the Gallup Organization, the percentage of Americans donating to charity with $100,000 or more in household income was 87 percent. The percentage in the $40,000–$99,999 bracket that gave to charity was 78 percent. Only 56 percent of households in the under $40,000 category reported making

---

8    Internal Revenue Service, "Ten-Year Change in Charitable Deductions by Income Level (2002–2013), Internal Revenue Service, Statistics of Income Division, Table 2.1 from 2003 to 2013," https://www.irs.gov/uac/soi-tax-stats-historic-table-2.

9    Emily Haynes and Michael Theis, "Gifts to Charity Dropped 1.7 Percent Last Year, Says 'Giving USA,'" *The Chronicle of Philanthropy*, June 18, 2019, https://www.philanthropy.com/article/Gifts-to-Charity-Dropped-17/246511.

gifts to charity.[10] The role wealthier households play in the market for charitable donations continues to grow.

Individuals don't support their church primarily to receive a tax benefit. In all likelihood, churches are somewhat immune from changes in tax policy. Churches may be the one charity donors will continue to fund. But a loss in a donor's ability to itemize could suppress member willingness to increase their financial support. The impact of TCJA is unknown, but it certainly could have a chilling effect on the ability of a church to grow its revenue base.

Interestingly, an increased concentration in charitable giving might, in the short run, prove to be a boon to some congregations. According to the 2018 U.S. Trust Study of High Net Worth Philanthropy, 90 percent of high net worth households gave to charity in 2017.[11] About half of these high net worth households gave to religious congregations and faith-based organizations. From a church perspective, the inclination of wealthy donors toward religious giving compares quite favorably to the general population, where only a third of Americans give to religious charities.[12] According to the U.S. Trust study, wealthy Americans are more likely to give to religion than average Americans. Churches with a wealthy membership may be playing on a field tilted in their favor when it comes to soliciting financial support.

For congregations with wealthy members, the news gets better. Religious organizations received the greatest share of high net worth charitable dollars in 2017, unchanged from a similar study conducted by U.S. Trust two years earlier. High net worth households gave 43 cents of every charitable dollar they donated to religious organizations. (Basic needs, the next highest category, only received 19 cents.)[13] High net worth households are more inclined to give to religion, and when they

10 Jeffrey M. Jones, "Percentage of Americans Donating to Charity at New Low," Gallup, May 14, 2020, http://news.gallup.com/poll/310880/percentage-americans-donating-charity-new-low.aspx.

11 The study defined high net worth households as those having a net worth of $1 million or more or annual household income of $200,000 or more, or both.

12 U.S. Trust/Bank of America Corporation and the Indiana University Lilly Family School of Philanthropy, "The 2018 U.S. Trust Study of High Net-Worth Philanthropy," Bank of America, 10, https://www.privatebank.bankofamerica.com/articles/2018-us-trust-study-of-high-net-worth-philanthropy.html, accessed January 27, 2021.

13 Ibid., 16.

do give, they give a disproportionately large amount of each dollar to religion. Churches with high net worth members should be well positioned to benefit from the increasing concentration of wealth that has been taking place since the turn of the new millennium.

For the vast majority of churches, however, the combination of declining membership and increasing wealth concentration are a cautionary tale. A shrinking pool of members/donors amplifies the importance of maintaining support from a handful of wealthier members. Yesterday's 80/20 rule (80 percent of the dollars come from 20 percent of the membership) that governed church fundraising efforts have become the 90/10 or even 95/5 rule in the new millennium. The financial implications of losing the support of a church's biggest donors through dissatisfaction, relocation, or death could be devastating.

### Cheese Insurance

Adopting a more rigorous and transparent approach toward monitoring and reporting church financial performance is not a panacea. There is no guarantee that a more rigorous program of analysis and communication of results will help maintain church revenue. And there are potential drawbacks if a more quantitative approach is not applied thoughtfully. As Jerry Muller cautions, "Used properly, measurement can be a good thing. So can transparency. But they can also distort, displace, distract, and discourage."[14]

Muller's concern is that while a quantitative approach can be valuable, the indiscriminate application of metrics management can be dangerous. Numbers are no panacea, particularly in a church context. As Muller explains:

> What can be measured is not always what is worth measuring; what gets measured may have no relationship to what we really want to know. The costs of measuring may be greater than the benefits. The things that get measured may draw effort away from the things we really care about. And measurement may

---

14 Jerry Z. Muller, *The Tyranny of Metrics* (Princeton, NJ: Princeton University Press, 2018), 4.

provide us with a distorted knowledge—knowledge that seems solid but is actually deceptive.[15]

Whether or not metrics management is a good thing in itself, as a general matter, donors expect to receive more quantitative information from the nonprofits they support. A growing number of secular nonprofits are embracing a results-driven approach to manage the relationship with their supporters. Donor expectations, particularly among wealthier donors, about the kinds of information they receive are changing. Does this mean that churches must follow suit?

The Giving USA Foundation, when analyzing American philanthropy in 2019, asserted, "Giving to religion has always received the largest share of giving and continues to grow at a slow but steady rate."[16] Individuals provided the vast majority (69 percent) of all donations in 2019 and, according to the National Study of Congregations' Economic Practices, individuals provided the vast majority (81 percent) of a typical church's revenues. On a macro level, religious giving was stable in 2019 and the economic engine of church support (individual donors) was running smoothly.

These statistics mask other important developments: religious giving has decreased over the last thirty years from around 50 percent of total giving in the 1980s to under 30 percent in 2019.[17] This is, in part, a product of the decline over the same period in religious affiliation and attendance. When these factors are considered in light of the increasing concentration of charitable giving among fewer donors, on a macro level it seems probable that the average church is becoming more dependent on donors who may care about metrics and performance.

Unfortunately, reliable information regarding the giving priorities of church members is unavailable. All charities are not equal in the eyes of all donors. If supporting church remains a high priority for the average church member, gifts may still be forthcoming even in the face of serious personal financial challenges. And macro trends, it should

---

15 Ibid., 3.

16 Giving USA Foundation, *Giving USA 2020: The Annual Report on Philanthropy for the Year 2019* (Chicago: Giving USA Foundation, 2020), 158.

17 King, Munn, Fulton, and Goodwin, "National Study of Congregations' Economic Practices," 14.

be noted, are just trends. The interest (or indifference) of the significant donors to your church in getting more financial and performance information is all that really matters.

It's possible that donor concentration and changing expectations among the wealthiest donors won't affect giving to churches. More importantly, it's possible this won't happen in your church. Perhaps your church members, particularly wealthier members, will forever embrace a kind of cognitive dissonance when it comes to contributions. They'll give because they believe in the mission. The information and communications they require from your church will be different from the information and communications they receive from the local food bank, hospital, or charter school. Over the next ten years, you will be able to find new church members with a similar attitude when your current members leave, die, and relocate.

Your congregation may very well buck these trends. On average, however, church members will expect to receive information from their church much like the information they receive from the other nonprofit organizations they support. When their church asks them to increase their financial support, in the absence of information that their church is achieving its mission, will they respond generously? Would they respond more generously today if the potential impact of their gift could be quantified? Would they respond more generously tomorrow if the church could demonstrate tangible progress toward the goals it has established and shared in an open and transparent way?

## Summary

The philanthropic ecosystem today is different from the one that existed at the beginning of the new millennium. A series of cultural, financial, and regulatory developments combined to change how very wealthy individuals engaged in philanthropy. Over time, these behaviors migrated throughout the philanthropic world, eventually reaching into remote corners.

Churches, for the most part, were untouched by these developments initially. The reasons church members give to their church may overlap, but are not identical to the reasons donors give to secular nonprofit organizations. For scriptural and other reasons, churches may have been insulated from these developments because church members privilege giving to their church above other worthy causes. Unfortunately, the pool of households capable of making substantial donations to any nonprofit is shrinking. This concentration of wealth into fewer hands means the average nonprofit—including the average church—is becoming reliant on a decreasing number of donors.

As competition for a shrinking pool of donors heats up, donors' expectations regarding the kind of attention they should receive has changed. Donors—particularly wealthy donors—have become accustomed to receiving increasingly sophisticated information about the activities of the organizations they support. This not only involves transparent reviews of operating and financial results of the organization itself, but comparative information so that the donor better understands the relative contribution the organization is making.

Church leaders may conclude that their church will remain unaffected by these developments. If members of their congregation make and will continue to make gifts to the church independent of national trends demanding greater transparency and accountability, their church can pursue a low output, traditional relationship with donors. A decision to continue past practices, however, is still a decision. If the composition of the congregation is changing, the consequences of ignoring these trends could have far-reaching consequences.

### Questions to Consider

1. What percentage of your church's total contributions came from the top ten households this year?

2. Does the inability to itemize contributions affect the amount a donor gives to their church?

3. How does the approach of your church toward donor communications compare to the approach taken by other nonprofits in your community?

# 7 · Generational Considerations

> Get rid of the old yeast, so that you may be a new
> unleavened batch—as you really are.
>
> —1 Corinthians 5:7

## Charitable Giving and Generational Preferences

Income inequality is a hot topic today. The increasing concentration of wealth into fewer households has implications for all nonprofit organizations that rely on charitable donations: fewer households will determine which organizations will survive. If the capacity to give was the only thing that mattered, donor-dependent nonprofits might be tempted to cater to the giving preferences of only their wealthiest supporters. Churches, unfortunately, are not immune from this trend.

Although the capacity to give is an important consideration, there are additional factors all nonprofit organizations must take into account. Donors from different generations don't want to interact with charities in the same ways. Younger donors respond best to appeals for support premised on the idea that their donation will make a difference. Younger donors want frequent, more metrics-based information from the charities they support. Younger donors are comfortable with digitally mediated forms of giving. The ways in which younger donors want to engage in philanthropy may overlap with those of older members, but they are not identical. A church that wants to ensure it has a sustainable revenue base must take into account not only the capacity to give, but generational factors that influence a donor's inclination to give.

Philanthropic engagement in a church setting involves more than just money. Church members also make gifts of time and talent, and member activity can have a material impact on the amount of financial support offered. In this book, we concern ourselves primarily with how and why members make financial gifts to their church. Yet it's important to acknowledge that philanthropic engagement involves all facets of church member relationship with their church.

Generational preferences influence church health more than anyone realizes. In a recent national survey, 85 percent of congregations with majorities of members born between 1965 and 1980 reported they were experiencing high revenue growth. Similarly, 55 percent of congregations with majorities of members born between 1946 and 1964 reported high growth in revenue.[1] Does this mean revenue growth is a cause or consequence of attracting a certain age group? The interplay between the median age of a church's membership and its financial health is complex, but one thing is certain: generational attitudes concerning charity and philanthropic engagement matter and deserve further exploration.

## The Generations Defined

Generations are social constructs. They have porous borders and cannot be defined with precision. Nonetheless, individuals born in certain eras exhibit certain patterns of behavior. As a result, organizations dominated by individuals from one era often act differently from organizations dominated by individuals born in another era. These patterns are not hard-and-fast rules and don't apply to every organization. They can be helpful, however, in understanding the behavior of individuals and groups they dominate.

Pew Research Center categorizes today's generations this way: Matures or the Silent Generation (born 1928–1945); the Baby Boomer Generation or Boomers (born 1946–1964); Generation X or Gen Xers (born 1965–1980); and Generation Y or Millennials (born 1981–1996).[2] Using these parameters, Exhibit 7-1 provides information from the Blackbaud Institute on the size and key giving statistics for each generation as of 2017.

---

1   David P. King, Christopher W. Munn, Brad R. Fulton, and Jamie L. Goodwin, "The National Study of Congregations' Economic Practices," NSCEP, September 16, 2019, 14, https://www.nscep.org/wp-content/uploads/2019/09/Lake_NSCEP_09162019-F-LR.pdf.

2   Michael Dimock, "Defining Generations: Where Millennials End and Generation Z Begins," Pew Research Center, January 17, 2019, https://www.pewresearch.org/fact-tank/2019/01/17/where-millennials-end-and-generation-z-begins/.

Exhibit 7-1

**Generational Characteristics**

|  | Matures | Baby Boomers | GenXers | Millennials |
|---|---|---|---|---|
| Birth Years | 1928-1945 | 1946-1964 | 1965-1980 | 1981-1996 |
| Age in 2020 | 75-91 | 56-74 | 40-55 | 24-39 |
| Living Members | 29.9 MM | 74.1 MM | 65.6 MM | 67.1 MM |
| Estimated Donors in 2018 | 23.5 MM | 55.3 MM | 35.8 MM | 34.1 MM |
| Percentage Giving | 78% | 75% | 55% | 51% |
| Estimated Amount Given in 2018 | $29 B | $59 B | $33 B | $20 B |

*Source: Mark Rovner, "The Next Generation of American Giving."*

Churches have welcomed members of all ages since ancient times. Perhaps it comes as no surprise that today the majority of congregations (53 percent) surveyed in the National Study of Congregations' Economic Practices reported that no single generation made up more than half of their attenders.[3] In other words, the majority of churches aren't dominated by members from one generation. Congregational identity is always a reflection of doctrine, tradition, location, mission, program, clergy, lay leadership, staff, and the socioeconomic characteristics of its members. Generational characteristics are a function of the members who choose to embrace a particular congregation's identity—a consequence rather than a cause. Any conclusions about how the age of its membership influences a church must be made with caution.

As Exhibit 7-1 indicates, Boomers—individuals born between 1946 and 1964—are the largest generation alive today.[4] The sheer number of Boomers means that the giving potential of the Boomers dwarfs that of any other generation. Not surprisingly, Boomers dominate chari-

---

3   King, Munn, Fulton, and Goodwin, "National Study of Congregations' Economic Practices," 9.

4   I am acutely aware, particularly in mainline denominations, that Matures constitute a significant portion of church membership. Moreover, even in churches where Matures are not a large percentage of the membership, they may still provide a large percentage of donated revenues. In 2020, the youngest Mature was 74 years old and the average Mature was 82 years old. A donor relationship strategy built around Mature preferences would not lead to a financially sustainable enterprise.

table giving today. The gross dollars that Boomers gave to charity in 2017 exceeded the amount given by the next most generous generation (Generation X) by over $25 billion. As a practical matter, no church—in fact, no donor-dependent nonprofit organization—can afford to ignore Boomers and their preferences.

The number of individuals in Generation X (individuals born between 1965 and 1980) is smaller than the number of either the Boomer or the Millennial generations. Recent research indicates that Gen Xers lag the Boomers not only in dollars given to charity, but in giving rates. The combination of a smaller population and lower participation account for the massive gap in gross dollars contributed to charity by the Gen Xers compared to their older Boomer siblings. Based on this statistic alone, you might conclude that the average church needs to calibrate its fundraising efforts with its Boomer members in mind. Such a strategy is unlikely to create a financially sustainable congregation over the long run.

Churches must aggressively cultivate their relationships with Gen Xers. Gen Xers donated $33 billion to charity in 2017, a significant sum that was second only in gross dollars to the amount donated by the Boomers. The youngest Gen Xers, 40 years old in 2020, are just entering their prime earning years, and will have more disposable income over the next decade. In the not-too-distant future, Boomer mortality will take its inevitable course. The Pew Research Center projects that by 2028, the population of Gen Xers will exceed the population of Boomers.[5] By the time 2030 arrives, Gen Xers will supplant the Boomers as the generation that matters most when it comes to charitable donations.

The near-term opportunities for developing a sustainable revenue base are less promising among the Millennial generation. Harsh as it sounds, the probability that a church's revenue will increase meaningfully during the 2020s by developing policies that primarily appeal to Matures or Millennials is low. The midpoint of the Millennial generation has not yet entered their prime earning years and, as Exhibit 7-1 illustrates, Millennials are the generation least inclined to donate to charity and today give the smallest amount.

---

5   Richard Fry, "Millennials Overtake Baby Boomers as America's Largest Generation," Pew Research Center, April 28, 2020, https://www.pewresearch.org/fact-tank/2020/04/28/millennials-overtake-baby-boomers-as-americas-largest-generation.

Before fashioning a donor relationship strategy around generational preferences, a church must understand in detail the age distribution of its current membership. If a church's membership is dominated by one generation, the most appropriate response may be obvious. Most churches today are not dominated by one generation even if Boomer members provide the majority of the revenue. Church leaders interested in building a financially sustainable organization must think beyond what's required to fund next year's budget. Blackbaud Institute pulled no punches in its 2018 report on generational giving patterns, "The numbers carry an important message for fundraisers. In the foreseeable future, your organizations' financial well-being lies primarily with Boomers and Gen Xers."[6]

### Generational Imperatives

Optimizing the revenue profile of any church begins with accommodating the preferences of its current and prospective members. Churches from the same denomination pursuing a similar mission and located just a few miles apart from one another might craft very different strategies based upon the age profile of their respective memberships. It is critical that church leadership understand the composition of the congregation, and that whatever strategy it employs for philanthropic engagement reflect the unique nature of its membership.

In chapter 6, we considered the intersection of wealth concentration and philanthropic engagement. All things being equal, the average congregation is likely to become increasingly reliant on a handful of members to maintain financial stability. The average congregation will also become increasingly more reliant on its Boomers and Gen Xers to maintain and grow its revenue base. Not every individual gives according to generational norms just as not every wealthy individual gives according to income strata norms. Yet there is evidence that the members of the Boomer and Gen X generations want to engage in philanthropy in different ways. The question is: do wealth and age influence how individual members give to their church?

---

6    Mark Rovner, "The Next Generation of American Giving: The Charitable Habits of Generation Z, Millennials, Generation X, Baby Boomers, and Matures," Blackbaud Institute, 2018, https://institute.blackbaud.com/asset/the-next-generation-of-american-giving-2018/.

Virtually every study indicates that both Boomers and Gen Xers give to any charity for the same reason: to make a difference. Consequently, Give.org reports that the majority of people say they want information about how their donation is spent and the effectiveness of their donation.[7] A fundamental challenge for any church is to articulate to its members that, based on its results, their donations are making a difference because their church is making a difference.

The problem for many established churches is that their donor management strategy is centered on answering this question with the Matures, rather than the Boomers or the Gen Xers, in mind. Matures give primarily from a sense of obligation and loyalty. Their decision to donate to an organization comes from a conviction that they *ought* to give and they *ought* to continue to support the institution because they've supported it in the past.

If we translate that preference into a church context, Matures may not care a great deal about a church's financial state or operating results. Yet, like Boomers and Gen Xers, they want their gift to make a difference, but they don't require evidence. They trust the church is stewarding their gift appropriately and will do the right thing. Philanthropic messaging for a congregation dominated by Matures would worry more about cultivating a heightened sense of obligation than describing church performance metrics.

Matures are a low maintenance group. Their relationship with the church is tied to the institution itself, more than its good works. The challenge for the church is simply to reinforce the donor's sense of affiliation. Once the decision to provide financial support is made, the donor assumes the church will spend their contributions wisely. They don't require frequent updates. Financial and operating information is not necessary. If it is provided, it can be done on a retrospective basis in summary form.

Boomers and Gen Xers do not share the worldview of the Matures. Boomers, as a group, may be more inclined to respond to their church

---

7   Elvia Castro, Ezra Vazquez-D'Amico, and Rubens Pessanha, "Give.org Donor Trust Report: An In-Depth Look into the State of Public Trust in the Charitable Sector," Give. org, 2017, 4. https://www.give.org/docs/default-source/donor-trust-library/give-org-donor-trust-report.pdf.

from a sense of institutional loyalty than Gen Xers, but will not respond with great enthusiasm. A different set of ground rules for successfully engaging Boomers and Gen Xers is required. As Michael Moody, coauthor of *Generation Impact: How Next Gen Donors Are Revolutionizing Giving*, puts it, "The biggest consequence for charitable organizations is going to be that they've got to retool how they think about engaging major donors. The next generation wants to be much more closely involved in hands-on ways inside the organization. . . . That means that the organization is going to have to be more transparent with these major donors."[8]

## A New Approach toward Philanthropic Engagement

If a church wants to create a more authentic, more productive relationship with its Boomer and GenXer members for fundraising purposes, what might it look like? As a first step, church leaders need to build consensus in the congregation around the following four principles:

1. Agree on what matters
2. Measure what matters
3. Report the results in a transparent manner
4. Own the results

### Agree on What Matters

Church goals can be famously open-ended. God's call to serve humankind is not bounded by geographic limits or resource considerations, and the mission statements of many churches reflect this expansive mandate. Unfortunately, some church leaders use the aspirations proclaimed by a church's mission as an excuse not to set specific goals. They reason that the divine nature of the mission transcends benchmarks. Or that it's too difficult to measure qualitative goals. Or that measuring performance is time-consuming and a drain on limited resources. Whether or not these arguments have merit, that approach ignores what we know

---

8 Quoted in "How the Next Generation Is Changing Charitable Giving," Wharton University of Pennsylvania, February 13, 2018, https://knowledge.wharton.upenn.edu/article/generation-impact/.

about the preferences of the Boomer and Gen Xer cohorts that make up their congregation.

The first step is a rigorous review of the church's mission and mission statement. Is it a general endorsement of Christian principles or does it describe the unique call of this congregation? Is it an artifact of history, or does it speak to the aspirations of the current congregation at this point in history? Setting appropriate goals—and addressing the informational needs of the church's donor base—is impossible unless church leadership can develop a consensus on what the congregation is called to achieve.

*Measure What Matters*

Whatever a congregation believes it is called to do, Boomers and Gen Xers will want the church's results to be measured. In 2018 BBB Giving Wise Alliance published the results of a survey that asked individuals of all generations which factors determined whether a charity deserved their financial support. Three factors were cited by a majority of both Boomers and Gen Xers surveyed: how much the organization spent on programs as opposed to fundraising and administration; how successful the organization had been in achieving the purpose of its mission; and whether the organization produced an annual report on its activities and finances and makes it public.[9] If these results are translated into a church context, Boomer and Gen X members will care whether their church is efficient and effective, whether it realizes its mission, and whether it summarizes and reports its operating and financial results.

There are no good or bad metrics for a church. The most appropriate group of metrics is one that reflects the mission of the congregation. The key is to devise a series of metrics and apply them objectively. Management consultant Jim Collins, a Boomer himself, asserts:

> To throw our hands up and say, "But we cannot measure performance in the social sectors the way you can in a business" is simply lack of discipline. All indicators are flawed, whether qualitative or quantitative. . . . What matters is not finding the

---

9   Castro, Vazquez-D'Amico, and Pessanha, "Give.org Donor Trust Report," 36–37.

perfect indicator, but settling upon a *consistent and intelligent* method of assessing your output results, and then tracking your trajectory with rigor.[10]

Like budgeting, the process of discerning what matters and trying to measure progress may be more important than the outcome.

## *Report the Results in a Transparent Manner*

In a donor relationship based primarily on loyalty and obligation, the content and frequency of reporting doesn't matter very much. In the late twentieth century, when Matures provided the revenue base for most churches, church leaders didn't need to give serious attention to reporting results in a consistent manner. Matures assumed that church leaders were pursuing the church's mission prudently. Interim reports to the congregation were unnecessary. Detailed year-end reporting was welcome but not required. Reporting on performance was not an important element of maintaining credibility with a church's revenue base in 1990.

Telltale signs of this approach remain with us today. The National Survey of Congregations' Economic Practices revealed that while 92 percent of churches produced an annual report, only 81 percent shared the report with the congregation[11] A significant minority of churches that go to the expense and trouble of producing an annual report do not share it with their members! In a relationship based on loyalty, sharing results with church members isn't a high priority. In the near future, when Gen Xer engagement will matter a great deal, this attitude will become problematic.

How best to share a church's results is a topic where some tension between Boomer and Gen Xer preferences can surface. This tension arises over media preferences, not underlying content. Blackbaud Institute found that a significant percentage (30 percent) of Boomers relied on annual reports for information concerning the nonprofit organi-

---

10 Jim Collins, *Good to Great and the Social Sectors: A Monograph to Accompany Good to Great* (Boulder, CO: Jim Collins, 2005), 7–8.

11 King, Munn, Fulton, and Goodwin, "National Study of Congregations' Economic Practices," 23.

zations they support. A much smaller percentage (19 percent) of Gen Xers prefer to receive information through this medium. Cultivating an effective relationship with church donors isn't just about results, it's about how and where those results are reported.

As might be expected, Gen Xers are much more comfortable with digital media. Although Boomers and Gen Xers typically visit the website of nonprofits for information, Gen Xers are much more likely to conduct a Google Search on the organization. Gen Xers pale in comparison with Millennials when it comes to consulting other forms of social media, but they are still more than twice as likely to do so than their Boomer colleagues.[12]

The effect on the congregation regarding a church's financial and operational performance will be influenced by how it is shared. The most appropriate solution, even if it were practical, is not a shotgun approach of tapping into every available form of media. The most appropriate solution will be to distribute evidence that the church is fulfilling its mission—that it is making a difference—in ways that satisfy the unique needs of each congregation's membership. Generational preferences should inform church leaders as they consider which forms of media might best serve their members.

## Own the Results

Deciding what matters, measuring what matters, and reporting the results in a transparent manner are important tasks for any church. A comprehensive program of this sort is not just good management, it sets the table for financial sustainability because it caters to the preferences of the Boomer and Gen Xer members whose financial support is critical to maintaining and growing revenue. Assembling and reporting the information is not enough, however. The church needs to acknowledge what worked, what did not work, and adjust its plans accordingly.

Too often, church leaders adjust the congregational narrative to highlight only those initiatives that are functioning well. In the parlance of the investment world, they selectively disclose the results. Rather than describe what worked, what didn't, and how these results affect

---

12  Rovner, "Next Generation of American Giving," 15.

planning for the future, management and leadership focuses only on success.

Celebrating success is important for many reasons, not the least of which is that it builds donor confidence. People enjoy being associated with winners, and church members are no exception, yet many church leaders choose to tell only part of the congregation's story rather than transparently demonstrating what the church set out to do and what it actually accomplished. This is not a disease unique to religious organizations.

If clergy and lay leaders don't take responsibility for performance through candid disclosure, how can the congregation appreciate the challenges they face? Why wouldn't members interested in specific aspects of the church become territorial, particularly in difficult times, rather than consider the needs of the church overall? How can donors be confident their contributions are making a difference? A willingness to measure and report on performance is insufficient; it must be accompanied by a balanced assessment of how actual performance fared against the projections made by church leadership.

If a church's membership has a meaningful representation from the Boomer and Gen X generations, a commitment to measuring and reporting results in a transparent manner may be vital in maintaining financial stability. These donors want a more organic relationship with their church than their parents did. For these donors, building that relationship starts with quantifying how their financial support is—and isn't—making a difference.

## Summary

Sweeping generalizations about how members of a particular age group behave is a dangerous game. Even when a statement about the group is directionally correct, it will be wrong when it comes to some individuals. Generalizations concerning church members of a certain age are no exception to this rule.

As a group, individuals of a certain age—just like individuals of a certain socioeconomic class—will exhibit common behaviors. An appreciation for group preferences is useful as a church negotiates its relationship with its donors. Relationships with individual church members are primary, but group preferences do play a role. Generational preferences on philanthropic engagement are something church leaders need to keep in mind.

The Matures that provided the lion's share of financial support to churches toward the end of the twentieth century were a low-maintenance group from a church perspective. The Boomers who dominate the philanthropic ecosystem today have different preferences, and the preferences of the Gen Xers who will soon account for the majority of charitable giving are different still. Neither the Boomers nor the Gen Xers are likely to be satisfied with a passive relationship with their church. Church leaders need to decide whether sharing information on church performance in a transparent manner could help the church cultivate a generous response by their Boomer and Gen Xer members.

### Questions to Consider

1. If you sorted your congregation by generation, would the percentage of the membership look different from the percentage of contributions?

2. Which generations do the ten largest contributors to your church fall into?

3. Assuming generational preferences matter, and in light of your answers to questions one and two above, what three steps should your church take now to enhance the financial sustainability your congregation?

# 8 · Managing Crisis

Hear this, you elders;
   listen, all who live in the land.
Has anything like this ever happened in your days
   or in the days of your ancestors?

—Joel 1:2

## Financial Crisis and Scale

A financial crisis in a church, like success, has many fathers. Sometimes financial crisis is self-generative, i.e., that the financial crisis is brought on by financial missteps by the church. More frequently, a church financial crisis can be traced to events or behaviors that have little to do with money management. Quite often, the root cause has little to do with the church. The financial crisis is quite real, but the cause lies elsewhere.

How does a church find itself in a financial crisis? A church can certainly bring on a financial crisis through its own activities and policies—poor management, poor hiring decisions, inadequate controls, etc. Quite often churches are dragged into financial crisis by events entirely outside their control. In the first twenty years of the new millennium, the terrorist attacks of September 11, the near depression of 2007–2008, and the coronavirus pandemic of 2020 threatened the financial well-being of churches everywhere. None of these events originated within the sphere of church activity.

One reason many churches can't successfully respond to environmental dislocations is because of size constraints. Small organizations have fewer resources in hand to counter disruptions: they are at greater risk of falling into a financial crisis because the resources they have available to manage through the situation are typically quite limited. Recall that according to the National Study of Congregations' Economic Practices, the average revenue of the average church they surveyed in 2018 was just $169,000.[1]

The consulting firm Oliver Wyman published a study that same year on the financial health of nonprofit organizations operating in the United States.[2] The study was based on information submitted to the IRS on Form 990, so it did not include data from churches. Oliver Wyman discovered that 66 percent of all secular nonprofit organizations reporting to the IRS had revenues of less than $1 million. It turns out that the average secular nonprofit, like the average church, is small.

Because the majority of secular nonprofit organizations are small, just like the average church, the results from the Oliver Wyman study may be relevant to church leaders. The Wyman study discovered that America's secular nonprofit organizations are financially fragile and noted:

- 7–8 percent are technically insolvent
  with liabilities exceeding assets

- 30 percent face potential liquidity issues

- 30 percent have lost money over the last three years

- 50 percent have less than one month
  of operating reserves[3]

Financial crisis has become the normative state for many nonprofits. Churches that find themselves in a financial crisis have plenty of company.

---

1    David P. King, Christopher W. Munn, Brad R. Fulton, and Jamie L. Goodwin, "The National Study of Congregations' Economic Practices," NSCEP, September 16, 2019, 4, https://www.nscep.org/wp-content/uploads/2019/09/Lake_NSCEP_09162019-F-LR.pdf.

2    George Morris, Dylan Roberts, John MacIntosh, and Adriane Bordone, "The Financial Health of the United States Nonprofit Sector: Facts and Observations," Oliver Wyman, 2018, https://www.oliverwyman.com/our-expertise/insights/2018/jan/the-financial-health-of-the-united-states-nonprofit-sector-.html

3    Months of operating reserves is a financial metric particularly relevant to churches. The calculation involves taking a year's worth of the organization's expenses from the Statement of Activities, dividing by twelve to get average monthly expense, and dividing average monthly expense into the liquid unrestricted net assets the church has available to meet these expenses listed on the organization's Statement of Financial Position.

## The Global Pandemic of 2020

The global pandemic of 2020 gave many nonprofit organizations, including churches, an unwanted baptism into managing crisis. Organizations that responded successfully utilized some of the techniques described in this chapter. For churches, these typically included: increasing communications with key donors, asking those able to accelerate annual pledge payments, cutting expenses, seeking federal government relief under the Paycheck Protection Program, preserving cash, and moving giving programs online.

Every church was in uncharted water and religious leaders wondered whether, despite their best efforts, their organization could survive. The Lake Institute on Faith & Giving conducted a survey of churches and other religious nonprofit and philanthropic organizations in April–May 2020 to better understand what was taking place at religious organizations as hospitalizations crested. Just over half the Lake Institute survey participants responded from a congregational perspective (clergy, stay, lay volunteers). Early in the pandemic, initiatives centered around pastoral care to counter the effects of isolation, anxiety, and motivation. From an organizational perspective, almost half of the survey respondents reported that the biggest challenges in the next six months would be stewarding organizational finances and doing effective fundraising.[4]

The external shock administered by a global pandemic did take a toll on many nonprofit organizations. As this book goes to press in 2021, many have failed. Some survivors have reduced staffing and programs to the point where their survival prospects are dim. And although the names of churches appear on the lists of dead and near-dead organizations, donor confidence surveys sponsored by Dunham+Company offer church leaders reasons for genuine optimism.

Dunham+Company conducted national donor surveys quarterly during 2020 to gauge the effect Covid-19 was having on donor attitudes. In the first (April) survey, 28 percent of all donors said they would continue giving regardless of the pandemic. Of this cohort, the sentiment to maintain prepandemic giving practices was strongest among

---

4   Lake Institute on Faith & Giving, "Faith and Giving in the Time of Covid-19," IU Lilly Family School of Philanthropy, June 2020, https://philanthropy.iupui.edu/institutes/lake-institute/Faith-and-Giving-in-the-Time-of-Covid19.pdf.

those who attend religious services at least weekly. Dunham+Company conducted follow-up surveys in June and September. Although the number of households who claimed they would not change their giving practices eroded from 28 to 26 percent between April to September, the percentage of this very committed cohort who attend religious services at least once a week *increased* from 40 to 44 percent.

Interestingly, the percentage of respondents who attend religious services who reported they were facing a challenging situation grew from 24 percent to 27 percent between April and September. This compares to an increase from 22 percent to 24 percent for all donors. In other words, according to the Dunham+Company surveys, donors who attend religious services are experiencing greater financial stress than the average donor, but their commitment to maintain their charitable giving practices is increasing.[5]

## Three Phases of Financial Crisis

A financial crisis generally occurs in three phases. Each phase can be labeled according to the primary activity church leaders must take in response: preventing, managing, and escaping. The activities of church management and leadership, the range of potential solutions, and the sense of urgency that characterize each phase differ. And, like everything else in church life, there are no straightforward "recipes" that assure success. The most effective handling of each phase will be dictated by the history, tradition, and resources unique to each church.

### Preventing

The best way of managing a financial crisis is to avoid it altogether. Crafting a program of prevention starts with an appreciation of what makes a nonprofit organization vulnerable to financial crisis. This is an issue that has received a great deal of attention from social scientists over the last thirty years, largely in response to a study published by Howard Tuckman and Cyril Chang in 1991.[6]

---

5   All three surveys are available at www.dunhamandcompany.com.

6   Howard P. Tuckman and Cyril F. Chang, "A Methodology for Measuring Financial Vulnerability of Charitable Nonprofit Organizations," *Nonprofit and Voluntary Sector Quarterly* 20, no. 4 (1991): 445–60.

Based on their analysis of Form 990 information, Tuckman and Chang concluded that a secular nonprofit would be most vulnerable to financial shock if it had (1) fewer revenue sources, (2) insufficient net assets, (3) low administrative costs, or (4) low income from operations. A significant amount of additional research testing Tuckman and Chang's conclusions has taken place during the past thirty years. No one in academic circles seriously disputes the validity of Tuckman and Chang's original work. Subsequent studies have focused mostly on suggesting refinements that would improve the model's ability to better predict which nonprofit organizations are likely to experience financial distress.

Some of the inherent differences between secular and religious organizations limit the applicability of Tuckman and Chang's work in a church context. Chief among these is their call to diversify revenue sources. Tuckman and Chang determined that nonprofit organizations with different kinds of revenue sources were better positioned to weather disruptions than organizations reliant on fewer kinds of revenue sources. Most churches rely primarily on member donations and can't diversify away from this type of revenue source. There are, however, five lessons that church leaders who want to prevent a financial crisis can absorb from Tuckman and Chang's work.

First, Tuckman and Chang's work—and the subsequent research based upon their work—is based upon four financial ratios. Tuckman and Chang posited what mattered, reduced the list to a manageable number, and rigorously reviewed actual results against the metrics they selected. Church leaders should identify a reasonable number of operating and financial metrics, measure actual performance against them, and report the results in a transparent fashion. A metrics-centered approach would also appeal to the church's Boomer and Gen Xer members as we discussed in chapter 7. If the church does experience financial crisis, maintaining the support of these donors could contribute to a successful resolution.

Second, in terms of categories, most churches will remain reliant on household donations for the vast majority of their revenues. In fact, spending money and time trying to develop alternative revenue sources might send mixed signals about the church's mission, creating confusion within the congregation that could eventually breed another set of challenges. These practical considerations don't alter the fact that becoming reliant on too few households makes a church's revenue stream fragile. Church leaders should take personal responsibility for cultivating relationships with every household capable of making a $5,000 (and higher) annual gift.

This notion of cultivating relationships with wealthier church members may strike some readers as upsetting, perhaps even un-Christian. It is a reflection of economic reality, not poor theology. Every human being is equal in the eyes of God. Every human being is not endowed with identical gifts. Therefore, all *donors* are not equal in the eyes of a church. Gifts of any size should be celebrated and joyfully received. But church members blessed with an abundance of time, talent, and treasure are called to a high standard, as the parable of the talents in Matthew 25:14–30 makes clear. Those individuals who have been given much are called to return much. Taking the steps necessary to make this possible is not in conflict with the gospel.[7]

Third, churches need sufficient unrestricted net assets to weather disruptive events. The definition of "sufficient" is always congregation-specific. It will look remarkably different in a megachurch in urban Texas than in a small congregation in rural Tennessee. Sufficiency is not measured only by the amount of a church's total net assets, but by the church's ability to access a portion of its assets quickly. Liquidity, as the Oliver Wyman study demonstrates, is a critical component of sufficiency. Total net assets must include a significant amount of unrestricted net assets held in cash and marketable securities.

The accumulation of unrestricted net assets, as described in chapters 3 and 4, largely comes about through a church's ability to generate operating profits year in and year out. Church leaders must have the discipline to operate profitably and to retain a portion of what they save in a form that is readily accessible. Unrestricted net assets held in this form earmarked for emergencies are called operating reserves. Although there are no hard-and-fast rules governing the right amount of operating reserves for nonprofits, a commonly accepted rule of

---

7   The mandate is repeated in Luke 19:12–27 in slightly different form in the story of the ten pounds.

thumb is 25 percent of the church's annual operating expenses.[8] In the case of Any Church, this would equate to $275,000 (see Exhibit 3-2). The discipline and willingness of leadership to maintain an adequate operating reserve will affect its ability to confront a financial crisis.

Fourth, as explained below, a church in the midst of a financial crisis will focus primarily on reducing expenses. Unlike revenue, expenses are within management's control, and progress in reducing expenses is felt immediately. Running too lean in normal times makes the hunt for expense reductions in a financial crisis more challenging. Churches, like all social service organizations, spend most of their money on people and programs. Insufficient investment in church infrastructure during normal times restricts opportunities to reduce expenses during more difficult times. Although good stewardship calls for exercising prudence at all times, underinvesting in human capital not only threatens long-term viability of a church, it limits management's ability to manage through temporary dislocations.

Finally, churches that want to avoid financial crisis can't simply generate minimal operating income year in and year out. They must generate reasonable operating margins on a regular basis. Like all nonprofit organizations, churches build total net assets primarily by generating operating profit and saving a portion. A church must achieve a reasonable margin, or the amount of dollars that actually find their way on to the Statement of Financial Position will be too small to counter any crisis. A church that consistently operates in the black is heading in the right direction, but unless that church operates with reasonable margins, it isn't insulating itself against financial crisis.

## Managing

Church leaders that want to chart a successful course through financial crisis must do three things. They must learn how to break eggs, act with urgency, and focus on liquidity. As Peter Drucker said, "The greatest danger in times of turbulence is not the turbulence, it is to act with

---

8 The Nonprofit Operating Reserves Initiative Workgroup, "The Nonprofit Operating Reserves Initiative," The Urban Institute, June 2016, 1, 3, https://www.nonprofitaccounting basics.org/sites/default/files/03-BriefIntroToOperatingReservesInitiative2016-06.pdf.

yesterday's logic."[9] The skills and resources required for operating in a financial crisis are different from those required in normal times.

Churches are notoriously reactive organizations. Churches often attract and hire individuals with a passive management style. Surviving a financial crisis requires a very different skill set than one that may have served the organization well in more prosperous times. To paraphrase Jim Collins, church leaders must get the right people on the bus, the wrong people off the bus, and get the right people in the right seats to transform an enterprise.[10] Some people will adapt and rise to the occasion, but church leaders may have to make very difficult decisions about staff once a church enters a financial crisis.

Crisis management requires intense, unremitting focus on financial details. It demands great patience and can be very frustrating. Progress is slow. In the short run, it's hard to tell if genuine progress is being made. And there are no silver bullets: success is determined by hundreds of small moves rather than a few large ones. The situation calls not only for a different kind of personality, but for a different kind of approach. Managing crisis requires such a radical change in the way the church operated previously that it sometimes precipitates a change in church leadership, church staff, or some combination of both.

Managing a financial crisis requires an openness to experimentation. Church management and church leaders must try a range of initiatives, many of which will fail or not produce the desired results. Experiments must be evaluated quickly and those that aren't working must be abandoned. This means quantifying and recording the results, even if the initiative doesn't easily lend itself to quantitative analysis. Most importantly, any lessons from failed initiatives must be processed quickly so they can help guide decisions about future experiments.

Actively managing short-term liquidity is always key to surviving a financial crisis. Developing and updating on a weekly basis a twelve-week cash forecast is particularly helpful in managing liquidity.

---

9    https://quotefancy.com/quote/887806/Peter-F-Drucker-The-greatest-danger-in-times-of-turbulence-is-not-the-turbulence-it-is-to.

10    Jim Collins, *Good to Great: Why Some Companies Make the Leap . . . and Others Don't* (New York: HarperCollins, 2001), 63.

Church leaders will find they have few revenue levers to pull, other than to encourage members to be as generous as their circumstances permit and pay any outstanding pledges as soon as possible.

Although no church can save its way to sustainability, managing through a crisis centers around rigorously managing expenses. Expenses, unlike revenue, are under management's control. There may be consequences for extending payments to creditors, but the decision to delay payment is within the church's span of control. The payoff from initiatives such as renegotiating supplier contracts may not be as consequential or as immediate. The aggregate impact of aggressive expense management is reduced pressure on the church's cash resources and liquidity reserves, which are so difficult to accumulate.

## Escaping

A church in financial crisis is, by definition, a church in transition. Hopefully, the congregation will emerge stronger from the experience. The only thing certain is that the church will not be the same community that entered into the crisis when it exits. The unique experience of each church makes it difficult to describe how to best position any church for returning to a state of normalcy. However, the underlying challenge for any church is the same: how do you establish and enforce financial practices that will enable the church to achieve its mission?

Harvard Business School's John Kotter conducted research on successful corporate transformations. In studying what actions lead to successful transformations, he also discovered what didn't work. Kotter lists eight reasons why the leaders of some of the companies he studied failed to transform their organizations successfully:

1. Not establishing a great enough sense of urgency
2. Not creating a powerful enough guiding coalition to effect change
3. Lack of vision
4. Undercommunicating the vision
5. Not removing obstacles to the vision

6. Not systematically planning for and creating short-term wins

7. Declaring victory too soon

8. Not anchoring changes in the organization's culture[11]

The companies Kotter studied were mostly large, for-profit enterprises. Yet his observations seem tailor-made for the leaders of a church mired in a financial crisis. The first order of business in a financial crisis is to survive the crisis. This requires a sense of urgency that is foreign to most churches, but it is a prerequisite to survival.

Mission (vision, in Kotter's terms) must become the centerpiece of any sustainable plan. Church leaders must coalesce around the mission and be able to explain why their actions will better position the church to realize the mission. Staff and the membership will be more inclined to accept difficult decisions if they believe those steps will contribute to realization of the church's mission.

A dashboard of operating and financial metrics that describe a church's performance is always useful. Perhaps having a set of agreed-upon metrics becomes most valuable when a church is working its way through a financial crisis and leadership begins positioning the organization for a return to normalcy. Quantitative goals tied to mission can help leadership counter emotional responses to new policies. Members won't welcome changes that affect their pet programs or threaten their spheres of influence, but they are more likely to accept change if it can be tied to a mission that they understand.

Addressing a financial crisis takes time. Even when progress is apparent to leadership, it may not be apparent to the wider membership. Small financial victories need to be targeted in advance and ought to be celebrated to maintain positive momentum. Finally, the new behaviors that lead to greater financial stability must be institutionalized. The best way to avoid future financial difficulties is to absorb the lessons learned from this crisis and make sure they become a permanent part of the financial infrastructure.

---

11 John P. Kotter, "Leading Change: Why Transformation Efforts Fail," *Harvard Business Review*, May–June 1995, https://hbr.org/1995/05/leading-change-why-transformation-efforts-fail-2.

## Summary

As described in chapter 1, faith communities inhabit an increasingly hostile world. The acidic effects of declining membership and reduced revenue have destabilized thousands of churches. More than ever before, church leaders must make sure they insulate their church from avoidable financial distress. Like any good fiduciary, they must be vigilant in rooting out waste, inefficiency, unethical behavior, and false reporting. Unfortunately, financial distress has replaced financial equilibrium as the new normal for many congregations.

A church in a precarious financial state finds it difficult to maintain daily operations. Fending off even minor dislocations can become challenging. When exogenous events affect a church, which they have with some frequency during the first two decades of the new millennium, a financially challenged church can quickly become a financially compromised church. It's not surprising that many congregations have become familiar with financial crisis over the past twenty years.

Preventing, managing, and escaping from financial crisis is a suit cut from whole cloth. The history, traditions, resources, and current leadership of the church will dictate how financial crisis is best negotiated in each local setting. Nonetheless, there are two ingredients common to the successful resolution of a church financial crisis: developing a laserlike focus on improving financial liquidity (including managing expenses) and linking major changes in activities or policies to the church's mission through quantitative measures.

### Questions to Consider

1. Does your church have a written policy regarding the creation and maintenance of operating reserves?

2. If your church had to reduce operating expenses 5 percent by the end of next month, what expenses would you eliminate?

3. Would a financial crisis make it easier or more difficult to talk about the linkage between money and mission in your church?

# 9 · Sustainable Church

> Now finish the work, so that your eager willingness
> to do it may be matched by your completion of it, ac-
> cording to your means.
>
> —2 Corinthians 8:11

## Is Church Different, Really?

If we set spiritual considerations aside, are churches structurally
different from other nonprofit social service organizations? Is there
something about their composition that renders any analogy we try
to make between the challenges a church and a secular nonprofit face
invalid? Is research based on the Form 990 information the IRS collects on tax-exempt organizations, which does not include information from churches, not really applicable to churches? Even if we know
a great deal about the structure and financial performance of secular
nonprofit organizations, does that knowledge give us insight we can
translate into a church context?

No one can speak with authority about the financial practices of
churches. There is no comprehensive, accessible data pool that con-
tains the financial and operating results of religious institutions.
Although pockets of useful information exist within denominations,
the amount and type of information each denomination collects dif-
fers, as do their collection methodologies. Even if the information was
comparable, and it was collected in a consistent manner, these data
pools cannot be freely queried. No one really knows what financial
practices work best for churches. Church leaders who want to assert
"You don't understand; church is different" can do so without much
fear of contradiction.

If we apply IRS nonprofit typology, churches are really a hybrid kind of enterprise, part 501(c)(3) charitable organization and part 501(c)(9) voluntary employee benefit organization.[1] When churches face outward, consuming resources to carry God's mission into the world, they look very much like certain secular nonprofit organizations. When churches face inward, providing services and programs consumed by their members, they look like employee benefit associations.

Churches march to the same essential beat as many secular nonprofits. Churches and secular nonprofits are driven by their mission rather than the creation of shareholder value. Churches and secular nonprofits have limited access to permanent capital. Churches and secular nonprofits must budget carefully, paying close attention to the liquidity of their unrestricted net assets. Churches and secular nonprofits rely on the same shrinking pool of wealthy donors. Churches and secular nonprofits are affected by the same generational factors. Churches and secular nonprofits regularly experience some kind of financial crisis.

Is church different, really? Not so different that the financial practices adopted by secular nonprofits and described in this book should be ignored by clergy and lay leaders. Not every one of these practices can be adopted by every church. (In fact, not every practice *should* be adopted; for example, Tuckman and Chang's call to diversify revenue sources.) If, however, a church's leaders are serious about mission, they should consider how the experiences of secular nonprofits can better inform their efforts to create a more durable financial structure to advance that mission.

## Sustainable Mission

Every new millennium church needs a compelling mission. Both the religiously curious and the religiously committed have plenty of alternatives. A church's mission articulates why it is in business, differentiating it from other religious and social service organizations in the local community. Consensus around a mission enables church leaders to make tough decisions during difficult times. Missions help members and staff keep their eye on the prize.

---

1  Employee benefit organizations are a collection of individuals and their dependents who come together on a tax-exempt basis for their mutual benefit.

Typically, the mission is reduced into a document called a mission statement. Given the primacy of mission, one would expect church leaders to devote significant attention to their church's mission statement. As is the case with secular nonprofits, church mission statements often get short shrift. Francis Pandolfi exclaimed in the Harvard Business Review, "As important as they are, mission statements are frequently little more than slogans. Many are lengthy and ambiguous or, to be useful, they must be accompanied by vision statements and lists of values, goals, principles and objectives."[2]

Pandolfi's prescription for what a nonprofit mission statement should accomplish is a call to arms for church leaders:

> An effective mission statement must be a clear description of where an organization is heading in the future that distinctly sets it apart from other entities and makes a compelling case for the needs it fills. Furthermore, this mission must be short, memorable and appropriate for a variety of organizational stakeholders including, for example, employees, funding sources, served constituencies and the Board of Trustees.[3]

Church leaders who want to create a sustainable mission should devote whatever time is necessary to crafting a mission statement that reflects the unique call of their church. Gil Rendle cautions this is a fundamentally different exercise than managing a church, "Discernment work is different from descriptive work. Descriptive work is present tense. It asks for clarity about the reality that currently is. Discernment work moves into the future tense to explore what should be and to explore our role in what is yet to come."[4]

Some church leaders will not be convinced that a mission statement really matters and won't fully engage. It seems too touchy/feely, a waste of time. Building consensus around a new mission statement can be

---

2   Francis Pandolfi, "How to Create an Effective Non-Profit Mission Statement," *Harvard Business Review*, March 11, 2011, https://hbr.org/2011/03/how-nonprofit-misuse-their-mis.

3   Ibid.

4   Gil Rendle, *Doing the Math of Mission: Fruits, Faithfulness, and Metrics* (Lanham, MD: Rowman & Littlefield, 2014), 88.

incredibly frustrating. Despite the challenges, mission statements are a necessary building block in the journey toward financial sustainability. Take the time to get yours right.

## Sustainable Financial Structures

Churches, like all other nonprofit organizations, are subject to the vagaries of accounting conventions. Accounting conventions aren't mere inconveniences; they have real-life implications. The most important one for church leaders to remember, from a sustainability perspective, is that accumulating unrestricted permanent capital is difficult and time-consuming. It is difficult because the primary way for a church to create unrestricted permanent capital is by generating an operating surplus. Church leaders must not only have the discipline to generate an operating surplus every year, they must save a portion of that surplus in a liquid form so that the church can respond to unexpected events.

Accumulating unrestricted permanent capital in a church is not only difficult, it is time-consuming. Because churches operate on thin margins, and because most churches are small, the gross dollars that the typical church generates each year as surplus are quite modest. A church that wants to increase its unrestricted permanent capital must be rigorous about adding to its capital base consistently because the dollars involved are small. This requires a robust budgeting process and the discipline to adhere to budgetary goals, year in and year out. Adding capital is not only difficult, it occurs at a glacial pace.

How much surplus is enough? Woods Bowman, a distinguished professor of public finance, suggests that any nonprofit's annual surpluses must be large enough to sustain financial capacity in all time frames indefinitely and to make additional investments for growth.[5] According to Bowman's calculations, the minimum annual surplus needed to maintain a nonprofits, capital base is 3.4 percent (the long-term rate of inflation) of total assets. A return above this rate enhances the financial integrity of the organization. A return below this rate will impair the financial integrity of the organization.[6]

---

5   Woods Bowman, *Finance Fundamentals for Nonprofits* (Hoboken, NJ: John Wiley and Sons, 2011), 156.
6   Ibid., 85.

What happens when a church does not generate an annual surplus? Is there really a problem when a church loses money once in a while? It depends on the membership's understanding of their church's mission and how their church fits into God's plan. If the church has a mission without a time limit, and most do, every generation associated with the church—past, present, and future—has legitimate claims to its fair share of the fruits of the organization. This is a concept sometimes known as intergenerational equity.

Clergy and lay leaders that oversee an operating loss effectively turn their backs on preserving intergenerational equity. They are privileging the rights of today's congregation over the rights of yesterday's and tomorrow's congregations. Why? Because the funds required to cover today's loss come from another generation of church members. When a church operates at a deficit, church leaders finance the loss either by dipping into the capital created by previous generations or by borrowing against the surplus expected to be created by future generations.

Intergenerational equity is hopelessly compromised when a church budgets for an operating loss. When a church *plans* to lose money, current church leaders are saying that their needs absolutely supersede the claims of other generations to the economic value of the church. They also excuse themselves and the current membership from making their own annual contribution to the church's accumulated unrestricted capital base. If the budget is met and the church incurs a loss as planned, they not only consume resources created by others, they write themselves their own hall pass, exempting themselves from adding to the total unrestricted net assets of the church.

## Liquidity

Shepherding an annual surplus from operations to become part of the church's permanent capital base is difficult and takes time. Church leaders must then take steps to assure the capital can be accessed when needed. Some portion of permanent capital must be held as operating reserves in a liquid form. Here again, nonprofit accounting conventions can be very confusing, making this critical responsibility even more challenging.

The permanent capital of a church consists of restricted and unrestricted net assets. Permanent capital—total net assets—can be thought of as the cumulative economic value of the church's mission since inception. Total net assets are not cash balances; they represent all of the assets that have been reinvested in the enterprise rather than consumed.[7]

Restricted net assets—true endowment—are easy to understand. Unrestricted net assets are a grab bag of sorts. Some of the value in the unrestricted net assets account is equity in fixed assets (for example, the portion attributable to the church building) that cannot be quickly turned into cash to meet an emergency or to seize upon an unusual opportunity. Although a total net asset account that is growing is a good thing, looking at that growth without a clear understanding of the component parts can promote a false sense of financial security. Church leaders must make sure the church maintains a reasonable amount of its unrestricted net assets in a liquid, immediately accessible form.

Understanding how much of a church's permanent capital is immediately available is even more difficult in congregations where a significant portion of their endowments are restricted. Endowments can be restricted by the governing body of the church or by the donor. Restrictions created by previous governing bodies can be lifted by the current governing body. Changing the restrictions on endowments imposed by donors rarely happens. If a significant percentage of a church's income comes from restricted endowments, and the restrictions don't allow the earnings to be applied to the church's current needs, the church's ability to pay its current obligations may be compromised. The mere presence of endowments is not a barometer of financial sustainability.

Church leaders need to create an operating reserve, setting aside a portion of unrestricted net assets that is immediately available to meet unanticipated expenses. The amount a church has available to fund an operating reserve is easy to calculate. Simply subtract from total unrestricted net assets the church's equity in fixed assets plus exist-

---

7   Thad D. Calabrese, "The Accumulation of Nonprofit Profits: A Dynamic Analysis," *Nonprofit and Voluntary Sector Quarterly* 41, no. 2 (2011): 302, https://journals.sagepub.com/doi/abs/10.1177/0899764011404080.

ing board-designated funds restricted for specific purposes. In other words, determine the cash and liquid investments of the church that are not reserved today for other purposes. Although a church's financial position and unique circumstances will always determine operating reserve policy, a general consensus has emerged that an operating reserve should be a minimum of three months of the annual budgeted expenses.[8]

## Metrics

The phrase "if you can't measure it, you can't manage it" is often attributed to management consultant Peter Drucker. It's a claim where some church leaders draw the line. When it comes to metrics, they argue, church *is* different. Metrics simply don't work in a church setting. Measuring and managing are appropriate for organizations designed to generate a profit, not for organizations intent on achieving God's mission. Missional objectives are real, but they are transcendental and therefore can't be quantified.

Drucker didn't say "if you can't measure it, you can't manage it." He said "if you can't measure it, you can't improve it."[9] Drucker's admonition can be embraced by every faith community that imagines itself a medium for bringing the Good News into a broken world. Gil Rendle articulates why churches need to quantify their mission and hold themselves accountable to metrical standards of their own creation. "The dilemma is that without measures of change—if we cannot have conviction that what we do actually moves us toward changing people and changing the world—our churches and denominations are left simply as places busy with their activities, worried about their resources and unsure if all of the activity and worry has any purpose."[10] Churches without metrical anchors may be doing great things, but they can't claim they are making progress toward fulfilling God's call.

---

8   The Nonprofit Operating Reserves Initiative Workgroup, "Operating Reserve Policy Toolkit for Nonprofit Organizations," The Urban Institute, June 2016, 17, https:// www.nonprofitaccountingbasics.org/sites/default/files/03-BriefIntroToOperating ReservesInitiative2016-06.pdf.

9   Zachary First, "What to Measure if You're Mission Driven," *Harvard Business Review*, July 2015, https://hbr.org/2015/07/what-to-measure-if-youre-mission-driven.

10   Rendle, *Doing the Math of Mission*, 81–82.

Rendle doesn't discount the difficulty of translating a church's mission into metrics. He goes on to say, "It is one thing to know our mission. It is quite a different matter to discern what is required first and subsequent steps must be put in place in order to move us closer to that central purpose."[11] There is no standard set of metrics that apply in every church context. The only rule, given the inextricable relationship between a sustainable mission and a sustainable financial structure, is that the list must be a combination of desired operating and financial outcomes.

Discerning which metrics matter is a journey that, when pursued faithfully, goes beyond traditional counting practices in church. For example, Mecklenburg Community Church (MCC) decided in 2010 that attendance figures were a poor measure for whether the church was succeeding in its mission of bringing people to Christ and growing their relationship with the church. MCC instead created a metric it labeled "active attenders." Active attenders are members who attend, give, or serve MCC within a six-month period. The active attender list is updated monthly, with individuals coming off the list if they do not engage within a six-month period.

MCC also maintains a membership list. Members are active attenders that make a series of additional commitments, including baptism, class attendance, and signing a doctrinal statement. Only members are involved in the production of worship services, assume leadership positions, or participate in business matters of the church. If a member falls out of active attender status, they are removed from membership. In 2014, MCC had 10,000 active attenders; the church set a goal of growing the number of active attenders to 20,000 by 2020.[12]

A 2020 search of MCC's website indicates the number of the church's active attendees remains at 10,000. MCC fell short of achieving the goal it set back in 2014. Anyone who concludes that MCC failed, from a missional perspective, misses the value of metrics. As Jim Collins says, "It really doesn't matter whether you can quantify your results. What matters is that you rigorously assemble *evidence*—quantitative or qual-

---

11  Ibid., 57.

12  James Emery White, "A Metric That Matters," *Christianity Today*, August 2014, https://www.christianitytoday.com/pastors/2014/august/metric-that-matters.html.

itative—to track your progress."[13] Deciding what metrics best reflect a church's mission and then bringing into place the resources required to realize the mission benefits a church in many ways.

## Transparency

The National Survey of Congregations' Economic Practices, as mentioned in chapter 7, revealed that 92 percent of the churches it surveyed produced an annual report, but only 81 percent shared their report with their own members. Assuming the NSCEP survey is representative of new millennium churches, this discovery makes clear that many churches have an opportunity to become more transparent. Transparency involves sharing information you don't have to share.

Why should churches become more transparent? One answer, covered in chapters 6 and 7, is that greater transparency is a prudent response to a changing philanthropic ecosystem. Today's wealthiest donors are conditioned to receive more detailed financial and operating information from the secular nonprofits they support. Younger donors whose support the church of the future will rely upon, including members of Generation X, want this kind of information as well. If for no other reason, churches need to become more transparent about their results simply to better engage present and future donor base.

Another reason churches should become more transparent is that the benefits of metrics management can be amplified when the results are shared with a church's stakeholders in a consistent and transparent manner. Church members have the information they need to be part of important conversations regarding the direction the church is taking. If members understand where the church is headed, they will better understand deviations from the plan required by temporary dislocations. For example, if a financial crisis develops, church members may be more willing to accept difficult decisions if they better understand the context church leaders are facing.

---

13 Jim Collins, *Good to Great and the Social Sectors: A Monograph to Accompany Good to Great* (Boulder, CO: Jim Collins, 2005), 7.

Finally, transparency is good organizational hygiene. It helps prevent church leaders from telling only part of the story or shaping the story into an optimistic narrative that justifies their actions. Transparency makes it more difficult to leave out important details that might affect some church stakeholders disproportionately. There is an old adage from the world of investments: "Good information travels fast, bad information travels slowly or never." Greater transparency helps assure that the essential information a church needs to realize its mission is available to everyone who needs it.

In *Measuring the Networked Nonprofit*, Beth Kanter and Katie Paine describe the process of becoming more data informed as a crawl-walk-run-fly evolution for most nonprofit organizations.[14] After deciding what success looks like and how it can be measured, the church begins collecting data, often starting with a pilot project. The process of becoming more transparent is similar. What to collect, what to retain, what to reveal, and which media to utilize is iterative. A good faith effort to become more transparent will inevitably lead a church down some dead-end alleys. The opportunity to improve communications and achieve better missional alignment is worth the effort.

## Summary

Churches, by their nature, are fragile economic propositions. The general demand for their product—religious services—has been on the decline for half a century. When the product is delivered on Sunday mornings, the risk of substitution is significant. Churches operate in highly fragmented local markets with few competitive barriers to entry. Consumers have plenty of options when considering how to spend their Sunday morning. And churches are highly dependent on these consumers for their income.

As if this weren't challenging enough, the accounting conventions that define the financial infrastructure of a church limit opportunities for capital formation. Fund accounting can obscure the actual availability of financial resources. In sum, the financial flexibility a church

---

14 Beth Kanter and Katie Delahaye Paine, *Measuring the Networked Nonprofit: Using Data to Change the World* (San Francisco: Jossey-Bass, 2012), 34–36.

has to fend off problems or take advantage of new opportunities is constrained in ways most members, including many church leaders, do not fully appreciate.

As the Nonprofit Finance Fund observed:

> There is a tension between the pursuit of mission on the one hand, and the maintenance of financial viability on the other. This concern exerts pressure on the day-to-day operations and decision-making at every nonprofit, and quite often, it seems as though one must be chosen in favor of the other. We would like to propose, however, that they must be weighed together. . . . The very health of the organization depends on it.[15]

It is disappointing when a secular nonprofit can't balance these competing forces successfully. People lose jobs, and constituencies are left unserved. When a church—an organization called to be God's arms and legs in this world—fails at this task, it is more than just disappointing.

Clergy and lay leaders must confront the reality of their current financial position without apology. By managing to metrics and through more transparent reporting, they can make the connection between mission and money more apparent to church stakeholders. They can meet the informational needs of current and prospective donors. Mission and money really are two sides of the same coin.

15 Clara Miller, "Linking Mission and Money: An Introduction to Nonprofit Capitalization," Nonprofit Finance Fund, 2001, https://nff.org/report/linking-mission-and-money-introduction-nonprofit-capitalization.

# Bibliography

## Articles

Bowman, Woods. "The Nonprofit Difference." *Nonprofit Quarterly,* January 16, 2020. https://nonprofitquarterly.org/the-nonprofit-difference/?utm_source=NPQ+Newletters&utm_campaign=8774c98db4-EMAIL_CAMPAIGN_2018_01_11_COPY_01&utm_medium=email&utm_temm=)_940663ald17-8774c98db4&mc_cid=b027560193.

Calabrese, Thad D. "The Accumulation of Nonprofit Profits: A Dynamic Analysis." *Nonprofit and Voluntary Sector Quarterly* 41, no. 2 (2011): 302. https://journals.sagepub.com/doi/abs/10.1177/0899764011404080.

———. "Testing Competing Capital Structure Theories of Nonprofit Organizations." *Public Budgeting and Finance,* September 14, 2011. https://onlinelibrary.wiley.com/doi/abs/10.1111/j.1540-5850.2011.00989.x.

Castro, Elvia, Ezra Vazquez-D'Amico, and Rubens Pessanha. "Give.org Donor Trust Report: An In-Depth Look into the State of Public Trust in the Charitable Sector." Give.org, 2017. https://www.give.org/docs/default-source/donor-trust-library/give-org-donor-trust-report.pdf.

Dimock, Michael. "Defining Generations: Where Millennials End and Generation Z Begins." Pew Research Center, January 17, 2019. https://www.pewresearch.org/fact-tank/2019/01/17/where-millennials-end-and-generation-z-begins/.

First, Zachary. "What to Measure if You're Mission Driven." *Harvard Business Review,* July 2015. https://hbr.org/2015/07/what-to-measure-if-youre-mission-driven.

Fry, Richard. "Millennials Overtake Baby Boomers as America's Largest Generation." Pew Research Center, April 28, 2020. https://www.pewresearch.org/fact-tank/2020/04/28/millennials-overtake-baby-boomers-as-americas-laregest-generation/.

Hansmann, Henry B. "The Role of Nonprofit Enterprise." *The Yale Law Journal* 89, no. 5 (April 1980): 835–902. http://digitalcommons.law.yale.edu/fss_papers/5048.

Haynes, Emily, and Michael Theis. "Gifts to Charity Dropped 1.7 Percent Last Year, Says 'Giving USA.'" *The Chronicle of Philanthropy*, June 18, 2019. https://www.philanthropy.com/articles/gifts-to-charity-dropped-1-7-percent-last-year-says-giving-USA/?cid2=gen_login_refresh&cid=gen_sign_in.

Internal Revenue Service. "Ten-Year Change in Charitable Deductions by Income Level (2002–2013), Internal Revenue Service, Statistics of Income Division, Table 2.1 from 2003 to 2013." https://www.irs.gov/uac/soi-tax-stats-historic-table-2.

Jones, Jeffrey M. "Percentage of Americans Donating to Charity at New Low." Gallup, May 14, 2020. https://news.gallup.com/poll/310880/percentage-americans-donating-charity-new-low.aspx

———. "U.S. Church Membership Down Sharply in Past Two Decades." Gallup, May 14, 2020. https://news.gallup.com/poll/248837/church-membership-down-sharply-past-two-decades.aspx.

Keating, Elizabeth, Geeta Pradhan, Gregory H. Wassall, and Douglas DeNatale. "Passion & Purpose: Raising the Fiscal Bar for Massachusetts Nonprofits." Boston: The Boston Foundation, June 2008.

King, David P., Christopher W. Munn, Brad R. Fulton, and Jamie L. Goodwin. "The National Study of Congregations' Economic Practices." NSCEP, September 16, 2019. https://www.nscep.org/wp-content/uploads/2019/09/Lake_NSCEP_09162019-F-LR.pdf.

Kotter, John P. "Leading Change: Why Transformation Efforts Fail." *Harvard Business Review*, May–June 1995. https://hbr.org/1995/05/leading-change-why-transformation-efforts-fail-2.

Lake Institute on Faith & Giving. "Faith and Giving in the Time of Covid-19." IU Lilly Family School of Philanthropy, June 2020. https://philanthropy.iupui.edu/institutes/lake-institute/Faith-and-Giving-in-the-Time-of-Covid19.pdf.

Letts, Christine W., and Allen S. Grossman. "Virtuous Capital: What Foundations Can Learn from Venture Capitalists." *Harvard Business Review*, March–April 1997. https://hbr.org/1997/03/virtuous-capital-what-foundations-can-learn-from-venture-capitalists.

Miller, Clara. "Capital, Equity, and Looking at Nonprofits as Enterprises." NPQ, August 16, 2013. https://www.nonprofitquarterly.org/2018/06/07/capital-equity-nonprofits-enterprises/.

———. "Hidden in Plain Sight: Understanding Capital Structure." NPQ, March 21, 2003. https://www.nonprofitquarterly.org/hidden-in-plain-sight-understanding-capital-structure/.

———. "Linking Mission and Money: An Introduction to Nonprofit Capitalization." Nonprofit Finance Fund, 2001. https://nff.org/report/linking-mission-and-money-introduction-nonprofit-capitalization.

Morris, George, Dylan Roberts, John MacIntosh, and Adrian Bordone. "The Financial Health of the United States Nonprofit Sector: Facts and Observations." Oliver Wyman, 2018. https://www.oliverwyman.com/our-expertise/insights/2018/jan/the-financial-health-of-the-united-states-nonprofit-sector-.html.

Myers, Marc. "A Perfect Game Inspired Dale Berra's First Name." *The Wall Street Journal*, May 12, 2020. https://wsj.com/articles/a-perfect-game-inspired-dale-berras-first-name-11589288739.

National Conference of Commissioners on Uniform State Laws. "Uniform Prudent Management of Institutional Funds Act drafted by the National Conference of Commissioners on Uniform State Laws and by it Approved and Recommended for Enactment in All the States at its Annual Conference Meting in its One-Hundred-and-Fifteenth Year, Hilton Head, South Carolina, July 7–14, 2006." Uniform Laws, November 8, 2007. https://www.uniformlaws.org/HigherLogic/System/DownloadDocumentFile.ashx?DocumentFileKey=d7b95667-ae72-0a3f-c293-cd8621ad1e44&44&ForceDialog=0.

National Philanthropic Trust. "The 2019 DAF Report." November 20, 2019. https://www.nptrust.org/reports/daf-report/.

The Nonprofit Operating Reserves Initiative Workgroup. "The Nonprofit Operating Reserves Initiative." The Urban Institute, June 2016. https://www.nonprofitaccountingbasics.org/sites/default/files/03-BriefIntroTo OperatingReservesInitiative2016-06.pdf.

Pandolfi, Francis. "How to Create an Effective Non-Profit Mission Statement." *Harvard Business Review*, March 11, 2011. https://hbr.org/2011/03/how-nonprofit-misuse-their-mis.

Pew Research Center. "America's Changing Religious Landscape." May 12, 2015. https://www.pewforum.org/2015/05/12/americas-changing-religious-landscape.

———. "The Future of World Religions: Population Growth Projections, 2010–2050." April 2, 2015. https://www.pewforum.org/2015/04/02/religious-projections-2010-2050/.

Randall, Rebecca. "How Many Churches Does America Have? More Than Expected." *Christianity Today*, September 14, 2017. https://www.christianitytoday.com/news/2017/september/how-many-churches-in-america-us-nones-nondenominational.html.

Rovner, Mark. "The Next Generation of American Giving: The Charitable Habits of Generation Z, Millennials, Generation X, Baby Boomers, and Matures." Blackbaud Institute, 2018. https://institute.blackbaud.com/asset/the-next-generation-of-american-giving-2018/.

Tuckman, Howard P., and Cyril F. Chang. "A Methodology for Measuring the Financial Vulvnerability of Charitable Nonprofit Organizations." *Nonprofit and Voluntary Sector Quarterly* 20, no. 4 (1991): 445–60. https://journals.sagepub.com/doi/10.1177/089976409102000407.

U.S. Trust/Bank of America Corporation and the Indiana University Lilly Family School of Philanthropy. "The 2018 U.S. Trust Study of High Net-Worth Philanthropy." Bank of America. https://www.privatebank. bankofamerica.com/articles/2018-us-trust-study-of-high-net-worth-philanthropy.html.

White, James Emery. "A Metric That Matters." *Christianity Today,* August 2014. https://www.christianitytoday.com/pastors/2014/august/metric-that-matters.html.

## Books

Bowman, Woods. *Finance Fundamentals for Nonprofits*. Hoboken, NJ: John Wiley and Sons, 2011.

Chaves, Mark, and Alison Eagle. *Religious Congregations in 21st Century America: National Congregations Study 2015*. Chicago: Giving USA Foundation, 2015.

Collins, Jim. *Good to Great: Why Some Companies Make the Leap . . . and Others Don't*. New York: HarperCollins, 2001.

———. *Good to Great and the Social Sectors: A Monograph to Accompany Good to Great*. Boulder, CO: Jim Collins, 2005.

Fulton, Katherine, and Andrew Blau. *Looking Out for the Future: An Orientation for Twenty-First Century Philanthropists. Cambridge, MA:* Monitor Company Group, LLP, 2005. https://community-wealth.org/ sites/clone.community-wealth.org/files/downloads/report-fulton-blau.pdf.

Giving USA Foundation. Giving USA Foundation, *Giving USA 2020: The Annual Report on Philanthropy for the Year 2019*. Chicago: Giving USA Foundation, 2020.

———. *Giving USA 2019: The Annual Report on Philanthropy for the Year 2018*. Chicago: Giving USA Foundation, 2019.

Hansmann, Henry. *The Ownership of Enterprise*. Cambridge: Belknap Press, 1996.

Herzlinger, Regina E., and Denise Nitterhouse. *Financial Accounting and Managerial Control for Nonprofit Organizations*. Cincinnati, OH: South-Western Publishing, 1994.

Ittleson, Thomas R. *Nonprofit Accounting and Financial Statements: Overview for Board, Management, and Staff*. Rev. 2nd ed. Cambridge: Mercury Group Press, 2017.

Kanter, Beth, and Katie Delahaye Paine, *Measuring the Networked Nonprofit: Using Data to Change the World.* San Francisco: Jossey-Bass, 2012.

Keucher, Gerald W. *Remember the Future: Financial Leadership and Asset Management for Congregations.* New York: Church Publishing, 2006.

Muller, Jerry Z. *The Tyranny of Metrics.* Princeton, NJ: Princeton University Press, 2018.

Nouwen, Henri. *A Spirituality of Fundraising.* Nashville, TN: Upper Room Books, 2010.

Rendle, Gil. *Doing the Math of Mission: Fruits, Faithfulness, and Metrics.* Lanham, MD: Rowman & Littlefield, 2014.

Robinson, Kerry Alys. *Imagining Abundance.* Collegeville, MN: Liturgical Press, 2014.

Wariboko, Nimi. *Accounting & Money for Ministerial Leadership.* Eugene, OR: Wipf & Stock, 2013.

Wimberly, John W., Jr. *The Business of the Church: The Uncomfortable Truth That Faithful Ministry Requires Effective Management.* Herndon, VA: Alban Institute, 2010.

## Podcasts

"How the Next Generation Is Changing Charitable Giving," https://knowledge.wharton.upenn.edu/article/generation-impact/.

## Websites

www.councilofnonprofits.org

www.fasb.org

www.irs.gov

www.mecklenburg.org

news.gallup.com

quotefancy.com